Wild cats, domestic cats, roaring cats, purring cats—here is the cat family from a weasel-like member millions of years ago to today's well-loved house cat.

After introducing the wild cats, including the lion, cheetah, jaguar, and bobcat, Carl Burger discusses in detail the domestic cat, a favorite companion of man from the time of ancient Egypt. With admiration and affection he writes about the breeds, the personality, and the place in history of this graceful, independent animal.

All About Cats

ALL ABOUT

Cats

BY CARL BURGER

ILLUSTRATED WITH PHOTOGRAPHS

with a foreword by William Bridges

RANDOM HOUSE   NEW YORK

PHOTOGRAPH CREDITS: The British Museum, 74, 77; Jane Burton (from Photo Researchers Ltd.), 57; David Cain (from Photo Researchers), 5; Walter Chandoha, endpapers, 1, 16, 89, 90, 99, 101, 107, 108, 111, 113, 115, 116, 145; John Gajda (from Alpha), 7; Bernhard Grzimek (from Tierbilder Okapia), 55; Thurston Hopkins (from Pix), 65; Hans Jesse (from Alpha), 131, (from Black Star), 125; Tommy Lark (from Photo Researchers), 46; Nina Leen (from Pix), 122; Al Lowry (from FPG), ii; Terence O. Mathews (from Photo Researchers), 23; Ben McCall (from Alpha), 18; The Metropolitan Museum of Art (Gift of Mrs. Florence Blumenthal, 1934), 70, (Rogers Fund, 1944), 2; Charles J. Ott (from National Audubon Society), 48; Chris Reeberg (from FPG), 11; Eleanor Rost (from Shostal), cover; Leonard Lee Rue III (from Annan), 53, (from FPG), 14, (from Monkmeyer), 21, 33; Antonio Serafini (from Pix), 78; Bud Smith (from FPG), 83; The Smithsonian Institution, 38; South African Tourist Corporation, 40; C. A. Spinage (from Annan), 29; W. Suschitzky, 25, (from Pix), 93, 118, 133; Louise Van der Meid (from FPG), 61; R. Van Nostrand (from National Audubon Society), 35, 43, (from Photo Researchers), 56; Joe Van Wormer (from Photo Researchers Ltd.), 51; Stan Vogel (from Photo Researchers), 10; Jeanne White (from National Audubon Society), i, 68; Stanley Zamenski (from FPG), 105.

The illustration on page 84 is from *The Wonderful Discovery of the Witchcrafts of Margaret and Philip Flower* (London, 1619), courtesy of the New York Public Library.

CONTENTS

ACKNOWLEDGMENTS

The author and the publisher wish to express their gratitude to the many scientific authorities and plain cat fanciers who have given valuable advice in the writing of this book.

The staff of the Bronx Zoological Park in New York have been most generous in contributing their time and expert knowledge. Especially helpful have been Mr. William Bridges, Curator of Publications (Retired), and Miss Grace Davall, Assistant Curator of Birds and Mammals.

Dr. James W. Atz, formerly of the Department of Animal Behavior, now Assistant Curator of the Department of Ichthyology, American Museum of Natural History, has given invaluable advice on the chapter discussing the mind of the cat.

Mr. Lee Crandall, General Curator Emeritus of the Bronx Zoo, has examined the chapters on the wild cats, and Mr. Raymond Smith, Editor of *Cats* Magazine, has read the chapters on domestic cats. Their comments have been most valuable in the matter of technical accuracy. If there are any errors on this score in the book, they are the fault of the author.

A final word of thanks goes to the staffs of the public libraries of Chappaqua, N. Y., and Pleasantville, N. Y.

FOREWORD

You can't be around a zoo very long without noticing something: people love the cats, big or little. They may laugh at the monkeys, pretend to shudder at the snakes, goggle at the brilliant birds. But let a wobbly lion cub make an appearance, and you might as well close up the rest of the zoo for the day.

This affectionate interest is not confined to zoo-going adults. Why does one children's zoo keep a padlock on its cat-and-kitten exhibit? Because loving children want to carry the kittens home.

In view of this enthusiasm, I foresee a loud purr of appreciation for Carl Burger's story of cats wild and domestic. After a few catlike leaps into and out of some especially dramatic periods in the history of domestic cats, Mr. Burger starts at the beginning some millions of years ago. He works steadily forward into the wild species of the present day and then spreads out with a most interesting account of domestic breeds. It is true that few of us keep the wild species as pets (none of us *should*), but they and even their remotest extinct ancestors tell us something about our household tabbies and their independent ways. Not much, perhaps, but something —for who is ever going to understand a cat completely?

Many have tried, and the more philosophical among us will read Mr. Burger's final chapter, "The Mind of the Cat," with emotions in which admiration for his impartiality struggles with our own bias. I am glad he stresses the point that we cannot judge the actions of cats by human standards; too many people do, for good or bad. One thing, though, we *can* agree on:

"Amid the anxieties of modern life, man needs the restful companionship of friendly animals. This need is well filled by the cat, the most beautifully perfect of all the animal kingdom."

WILLIAM BRIDGES
Curator of Publications (Retired)
New York Zoological Society

All About Cats

CHAPTER 1

Ups and Downs of an Old Family

It is a spring day some three thousand years ago. The great temple of Bubastis, on an island in the Nile delta, is crowded with worshipers. They have come here from all parts of Egypt to celebrate the annual festival of Pasht, the cat goddess. Many have traveled by boat, bringing along their musical instruments, for this is a joyful celebration. On their way they have stopped at various wharves along the river to serenade the villagers.

In the inner shrine of the temple, surrounded by tall columns, the huge stone statue of the goddess sits serenely on a throne. Her body is carved in the form of a woman, but her head is the head of a cat.

Pasht is one of the most powerful and revered of the many Egyptian deities, and the people bow reverently before her. Priests lay rich offerings at her feet: meat, honey, oils, and

3

A bronze statue made by an Egyptian artist 2500 years ago.

fruit. A group of flower-bedecked maidens sing as they dance around the statue, waving rattles to sound a shrill rhythm. Some of them carry censers from which flow clouds of fragrant incense.

Near the statue and elsewhere in the great hall, many cats prowl in the shadows, their eyes shining in the half light. Wherever one of their bodies catches a ray of sun, its sleek coat glints and shimmers. These are the temple cats, the sacred companions of the goddess. Priests tenderly care for them throughout their lives. In the eyes of the worshipers, they are scarcely less sacred than the goddess.

Another scene presents a very different picture of the regard in which cats were held in a later time.

The year is 1575 A.D. In a small city of northern France, the feast of Saint John is being celebrated. Last night was Saint John's Eve, the time when all witches and wizards of the surrounding countryside are believed to assemble for an annual convention, or Sabbath. Accompanied by their cats, they are thought to have met with Satan, their master, to receive his orders, to hatch plots against mankind in general, and to cast spells over their particular enemies.

The superstitious citizens of the town, as well as many other people of the time, believe that on Saint John's Day they must take drastic measures to counteract the evil schemes concocted by the witches on the previous evening.

The streets are crowded with gaily dressed merrymakers.

Processions move along the avenues, the marchers carrying lanterns and torches. Musicians entertain the assemblage with rollicking tunes. Laughing and screaming children dance hand in hand.

As the huge bonfire in the principal square blazes high, a group of men approach it. Each carries a closed wicker-work basket in which crouches a miaowing cat. The people believe that these animals are in league with the

powers of darkness; they must be destroyed in order to foil the dark conspiracies of the witches, their masters.

At a signal, each man tosses his basket into the blazing flames. The onlookers shout their loudest, and the dancers increase their frenzy. Having destroyed the witches' allies, the townspeople believe they can rest easy during the coming year, relatively safe from the wicked designs of Satan.

On the following morning, one Lucas Pommoreux, the city's official cat catcher, will appear at the town hall to receive generous pay from tax funds for having supplied "all the cats needed for the fire on Saint John's Day."

This barbarous celebration will be repeated each year until 1604, when King Henry IV is persuaded by his young son and heir to forbid it.

Now we go to a happier scene of our own time. In the kitchen of a comfortable farmhouse, a child carries in her arms her particular pet, a well-fed, purring tabby. One of its legs is wrapped in bandages. A few days ago it slightly injured one of its front paws, which has been treated by an experienced veterinarian. The paw will soon be well, but now the cat limps as it walks. To save it pain, its mistress carries it from place to place.

The girl puts it down gently before a box in which another cat and her kittens lie on a soft bed of blankets. The mother cat purrs contentedly as the four little ones nurse. Then the two cats touch noses in greeting as their mistress strokes both

of them fondly. The girl's mother brings a pan heaped with food, sets it on the floor, and the two cats eat their fill.

These three incidents are typical of the changing ways in which cats have been regarded by the people of times past and present.

In the ancient civilization of Egypt, they were worshiped as gods. Not only the temple cats were held sacred; every cat in every home was revered as one of a race that were the intimate companions of Pasht. No one mistreated a cat in any Egyptian home, from Pharaoh in his splendid palace to the peasant in his humble hut.

In the minds of the superstitious people of later times cats had become devils, and no fate was deemed too cruel for them. They were beaten with flails to celebrate the end of harvest season, hurled from lofty towers during Lent, and considered to be the evil companions of witches and wizards.

In our times, pussy has come to be an honored and beloved house guest in countless homes. She is neither worshiped nor persecuted, but admired for her beauty and treasured as the pet of the entire family.

CHAPTER 2
Prehistoric Cats

An old tale accounts for the origin of the cat family in a thoroughly unscientific way. Not long after Noah had loaded the Ark with animals and set sail on his memorable voyage, he found that the vessel was overrun with mice. The original pair had multiplied so rapidly that their offspring were adding greatly to the discomforts of an already overcrowded passenger list. Even more serious were the terrific inroads the hungry rodents were making on the food supply. Noah in desperation went to the lion and asked his advice. After a moment's thought, the resourceful king of beasts took a deep breath, humped his back, and brought forth a mighty sneeze. Out from his mouth popped a pair of house cats! Needing no urging, they immediately went to work. Soon all but one pair of mice had disappeared. These Noah caught and confined in a cage till the end of the voyage.

A much more scientific account of the origin and history of the family of cats is told, at least in broad outline, by the record that fossils have left buried in the rocks.

All soft parts of an animal's body disappear soon after its death. But the bones, after ages of time and under certain conditions, turn into stone in the exact shape of the original skeleton. Then they are called fossils. By comparing many

In legend and in fact, the lion and the domestic cat are very closely related.

fossils from various periods in the world's history, experts can learn a great deal about the family history of any animal.

So long ago that we can scarcely conceive so vast an expanse of time, there lived a small, weasel-like animal that scientists call *Miacis*. Judging by its fossil remains, it was about the size of a skunk, had a slender body, a long tail, and rather short legs. Its feet were fit for climbing, and its teeth were useful for gripping and tearing flesh. *Miacis* was a member of the extinct family Miacidae, which gave rise to many of today's land-living animals that live mainly on meat and feed their young on milk from the mother's body. They are known as "carnivorous mammals."

As time went on, the descendants of *Miacis* split into various branches. Slowly changing through millions of years, these branches developed into animal families that we know today—dogs, raccoons, bears, weasels, civets, hyenas, and cats. (See Appendix, pages 134–35.) These creatures are very different from one another. But they all have these two characteristics in common: they all eat meat, and they all suckle their young.

Some thirty-five million years ago the first definitely cat-like animals branched off the line of *Miacis*. Early in the history of this branch, it divided into two distinct groups.

One group, the saber-toothed cats, developed into huge creatures with long dagger-like canine teeth. Their great strength, fearsome teeth, and sharp claws would seem to have equipped them well for a life of preying on other animals.

But none of them has survived to our time. They became extinct some twenty thousand years ago.

One of their last survivors was *Smilodon,* the fierce saber-toothed tiger, the terror of early man. This ferocious beast was more than a match for most of the animals that lived in its time. It probably did not dare attack the mammoth and a few others. Whether the cave man, with his crude weapons, was able to overcome it we do not know. But he certainly must have feared it. Its body, heavier than any modern tiger, ended in a short, stubby tail. The two knife-like canine teeth, growing down from its upper jaw, were eight inches long. They reached far below and outside the lower jaw. But it could open its mouth so wide that these huge teeth were completely exposed. They were probably used to stab the animal's victims.

The prehistoric cat-like animals in the second group developed into the many kinds of cats that now live on every continent except Australia. Modern cats differ greatly in size and outward appearance, but in their basic structure—their anatomy—they are very much alike. All have skulls of the same general shape, and the same arrangement of body skeleton. The bones form a wonderful system of springs and levers, which are powered by strong, bulky muscles. With such a combination, cats are unexcelled among all animals for the ability to jump and pounce upon their prey. All cats walk on their toes, not on the soles of their feet as we do. The teeth are ideally designed, the long canines for tearing,

13

The bones and muscles of a cat are ideally suited for jumping and pouncing.

and the others for shearing off chunks of flesh. No other animal is better equipped for the kind of life it leads.

The Animal Kingdom is made up of many FAMILIES, each with its own scientific or technical name. Naturalists use these names in writing about animals, and it is helpful to know their meaning.

The family of cats is named Felidae. It embraces all living cats from the majestic lion to the smallest domestic cat.

The family Felidae is divided into three GENERA, each made up of cats that have certain broad physical features in common. The genus (singular form of genera) of the domestic cat is *Felis*.

Each genus contains one or more SPECIES. The members of a species have close physical resemblances, something like brothers and sisters in a human family. The name of the species of the domestic cat is easy to remember. It is *catus*, which, as you might guess, is the Latin word for cat.

Each species is called by the name of its genus, followed by the name of its species. This is the same way that names appear in a telephone book. The technical name of your cat, then, is *Felis catus*.

You may be wondering why anyone should go to all this trouble to name a cat. Why not just call it a *cat*? In the first place, the name *cat* might refer to a leopard or a lynx or a tiger. They are all cats. The technical name *Felis catus* identifies your pet as a domestic cat and sets it apart from other members of the cat family.

Another reason for technical names is that they enable naturalists all over the world to know exactly what animal you have in mind. The word for cat in Spanish is *gato*, in German *katze*, in French *chat*, in Arabic *kittah*. A naturalist speaking any language other than English might not understand "domestic cat." But he would know what animal you

meant if you said *"Felis catus."* Technical names are a world-wide language among scientists.

While animals of different species do not usually mate with one another, sometimes this does occur. The offspring of such matings are known as hybrids. Our domestic cats are believed to be the result of mating between two or more species of the smaller wild cats. But their interbreeding occurred so long ago that naturalists now regard domestic cats as a separate species.

The various varieties of domestic cats—such as Persian, Manx, Siamese—are breeds, not species. A breed is the result of selective breeding controlled by man, while a species is the result of natural evolution through the ages.

17

TABBY CATS, *a variety of* Felis catus.

CHAPTER 3
Roaring Cats

Of the three genera of the cat family, we have already mentioned one: *Felis*. The other two genera are named *Panthera* and *Acinonyx*.

The genus *Panthera* contains six species: lion, tiger, jaguar, leopard, snow leopard, and clouded leopard. Known as the "roaring cats," they all have in their throats a powerful sound-making apparatus, corresponding to our "Adam's apple," which enables them to roar. When in the mood, they also purr. Jaguars and leopards make little use of their roaring equipment. The most gifted performer in that field is the lion.

The genus *Acinonyx* has only one species, the cheetah. Later on, we will see why it is the only species in its genus.

The genus *Felis* contains twenty-nine species. We will call them the "purring cats." It is not known that they all purr, but they all lack the powerful sound box of the roarers.

In the entire cat family, then, there are thirty-six species (listed on pages 136–37 of the Appendix). Twenty-three are natives of the Old World, and eleven of the New. One species of wild cat, the lynx, is common to both the Old and New Worlds. The remaining species, the domestic cat, has been distributed by man all over the globe.

In this and the following chapter we will look at the roaring cats and the cheetah. Chapter 5 will discuss some of the wild species of purring cats. The rest of the book will be devoted to the domestic cat.

LION

In historic times, lions ranged over the greater part of Africa, as well as Greece, India, Turkey, and Iran. Outside Africa, they have now disappeared everywhere except India, where a small remnant of some 250 animals lives in the Gir Forest, a government reserve.

In Africa, the lion's range has shrunk to include only the central part of the continent. Even there, their numbers are being rapidly reduced. Sportsmen shoot them for trophies. Native tribes spear them to make headdresses of the manes. Antelopes and zebras, the lions' principal prey, are much less plentiful than formerly, so that the big cats find it increasingly difficult to get enough food. A large male may weigh more than 400 pounds, and measure nine and a half feet from nose to tail tip. It takes a lot of meat to feed him. In central and southern Africa, there are several large government reserves where all animals are protected. These sanctuaries offer the best hope of saving the species from extinction.

Unlike other cats, which are usually solitary hunters, lions often hunt in small packs, called "prides." Approaching stealthily to within fifty yards or so, one of the pride bursts into a swift dash and leaps to the back or neck of its prey. It is usually a female that makes the final sprint and brings down the quarry. Then the whole pride join in sharing the meal. They have difficulty in chewing food, and prefer to swallow it in large chunks.

A LION, *his mate, and their two cubs.*

A pride is usually a family group, with one adult male as boss, several females with cubs, and perhaps a few young males. They all lead a quiet and peaceful life together, except during the mating season. The lionesses are generous with their milk, and do not object to nursing cubs other than their own. Hunting is usually done at night. The days are spent largely in idleness and sleep.

The reputation of the lion as a man-killer has been greatly exaggerated. By and large it is a peaceable, good-natured beast and does not attack man unless molested. However, it is dangerous when aroused or when, as sometimes happens, it has acquired a taste for human flesh. Lions once held up the building of the Uganda Railway for nine months, during which time they killed a great many laborers.

The cattle of native herders frequently fall victims to lions. The herds are protected at night in corrals enclosed by high fences made of thorny tree limbs. Simba (as Africans call the lion) occasionally jumps over such a fence and drags the kill back over it into the bush. This heavy animal can jump as high as twelve feet, and can leap three times the length of its own body. Though they can climb trees, lions usually keep to the ground. They can swim, but do not like to take to the water.

Cubs are born to the mother lion about 108 days after mating. Newborn cubs are thickly spotted. During their first few months they spend much time in boisterous play. From one to six cubs may be born in a litter, but the usual

Like a human mother, a lioness may become irritated with her offspring.

number is three or four. Cubs are carefully looked after by the mother till they are weaned, which occurs when they are about six months old.

At three or four years young lions are mature and ready to have a family of their own. In the wild, Simba may live from eight to ten years. In zoos, where there is plenty of good food and freedom from danger, the life span is usually longer. A male in the Bronx Zoo of New York lived fourteen years and three months. At that age, it was so decrepit that it was mercifully destroyed.

Because of their magnificent appearance, lions have been shown as exhibits for more than 3000 years. In captivity, they mate readily. Thousands have been born in zoos and have never known their native wilds.

There have been many cases of crossbreeding between captive lions and tigers. These hybrids are called "ligers" if the sire is a lion, "tiglons" if sired by a tiger. They are usually unable to bear cubs. However, a case is known where a female liger, paired with a full-blooded lion, gave birth to a cub. When grown, this cub produced five litters sired by a lion. Ligers and tiglons resemble both parents in color and markings, but are much larger animals.

TIGER

The tiger's tawny yellow coat, bold black stripes, and white facial patches mark him as perhaps the handsomest of the big cats. Unlike the lion, this is a solitary forest dweller that seldom ventures into open country. Rivaling or even surpassing the lion in strength and ferocity, it preys on most of the animals that live in its habitat. Not even buffalo and young elephants are free from an occasional attack. The chief items on the tiger's menu are deer and wild pigs, but it does not scorn lesser animals when hungry. It is a notorious killer of domestic cattle, and once in a while attacks a man. Like most cats, the tiger stalks its prey till close enough to make a final swift dash, which ends in a leap to the quarry. Most of its hunting is done at night.

This is the typical big cat of Asia, ranging from the Caucasus Mountains eastward to Siberia, and southward through the East Indies. It thrives both in the cold northern

TIGER

mountains and in the lush tropical forests of the continent. In India it is truly lord of the jungle.

The great Siberian tiger is the largest cat alive today. A big male may weigh more than 550 pounds, although the average is around 420. Females weigh considerably less. The smaller tigers of China, Thailand, and the East Indies are found as far south as the tropical island of Bali. Tigers do not inhabit the islands of Borneo and Ceylon, and there are none in Africa.

A tigress gives birth to her cubs from 100 to 109 days after mating. Litters consist of from one to four. Newborn cubs weigh between three and four pounds, and measure around twenty inches from tip to tip. Their eyes are closed for the first week or so. The mother cares for the young until they are weaned, and may live and hunt with them till they are fully grown. The life span, as recorded in captivity, is somewhat shorter than that of the lion.

In zoos, these beautiful beasts are invariably among the most popular of all animal exhibits. Especially at feeding time, visitors crowd around their cages to watch them devour from eight to twelve pounds of meat apiece. Tigers wolf down meat in large chunks. Their teeth are not well designed for chewing. As among all cats, the tongue is equipped with a very rough surface, used for rasping meat off the bones.

Tigers breed readily in captivity, but the female does not always prove to be a good mother. The Bronx Zoo in New

York was for years fortunate in being able to provide an excellent foster mother when one was needed. Mrs. Helen Martini, wife of the keeper of the Lion House, mothered many baby animals, both at the zoo and in her home. In the winter of 1944, three fine cubs were born to a tigress which had not succeeded in rearing any of her former litters. These triplets were turned over to Mrs. Martini, who fed them on evaporated milk mixed with water and vitamins from a nursing bottle till they were ready to eat meat. An electric pad kept them warm. The three grew up to be handsome, healthy animals in the zoo's Lion House.

At a little under four years of age Dacca, the only female, bore a litter of three. From earliest cubhood, Dacca had been particularly friendly with her foster mother, and now showed no anxiety when Mrs. Martini visited her young ones. One day Dacca came to the front of the cage carrying a cub in her mouth. Mrs. Martini put her hands through the heavy wire mesh that screened the cage's front. Dacca dropped her baby into the extended hands, then turned and started back to her den, evidently feeling that her offspring would be safe. When Mrs. Martini called out, the mother returned, took the cub, and carried it to join its two litter mates.

Up to the time of her death in 1964, Dacca had produced eleven litters totalling 32 cubs. Of these, 28 were reared to maturity, some by Dacca and some by her own foster mother. As young animals, they were placed in various zoos, either by gift or in exchange for other animals. Recently the Bronx Zoo set out to learn how the members of this numerous family had fared in their new homes. The most interesting report came from the Lincoln Park Zoo in Chicago. It showed that Bara, Dacca's twelfth cub, had bettered her mother's record for large families by one. Up to October, 1965, Bara had mothered fifteen litters totaling 33 cubs.

LEOPARD

The beauty of the leopard has led to its widespread slaughter. Its tawny coat, decorated with clusters of dark spots, is a fur highly prized among fashionable women.

An old name for any big cat, other than a lion, was *pard*. The Latin name for lion is *leo*. The two words were combined to make *leopard*.

The range of the leopard covers southern and eastern Asia and once extended throughout Africa. In the latter continent, it has disappeared from the countries along the Mediterranean Sea, and from the more settled parts of the south.

This is a stealthy, solitary animal, seldom associating with its own kind except when mating. Lying concealed deep in the jungle during the day, it stalks its prey by night. Its habit when hunting is to crouch in thick cover near a game trail, or to lie stretched out on a limb above it. When an unsuspecting animal comes near, the lurking cat springs upon it. Dense rain forests and jungles are its favorite haunts. It

LEOPARD

shuns the open plains favored by lions.

The victims of the leopard's hunting are sometimes larger than itself. A kill is dragged into the forest, where it may be hauled up into the crotch of a tree. Here the killer can enjoy a meal undisturbed by jackals and hyenas. Animals too large to be consumed at one sitting are left in the tree, where they will be out of the reach of scavengers. The leopard will return to its larder at another time.

Leopards are somewhat smaller than lions or tigers. They prey on almost any animal that can be attacked with a chance of success. Their favored food is any of the smaller deer and antelope. Leopards have a great appetite for dogs, and have been known to enter a hut, snatch a pet from under its master's feet, and beat a quick retreat. Baboons, which run in herds, are a frequent prey. But the cautious cats are wary of these animals. Occasionally a herd of angry baboons will surround a marauding leopard and tear it to bits.

Rather frequently, especially in India, a black cub occurs in a normally colored litter. Black leopards are not a separate species, but a color variation of the ordinary leopard. Their fur is jet black with the spots showing dimly in bright sunlight as areas of shinier black. Often called black panthers, in the zoo they are frequently named Bagheera, after Mowgli's companion in Kipling's *Jungle Books*.

Most African hunters agree that the leopard is the fiercest of all cats, the only one that commonly attacks man. Carl Akeley, a great naturalist and animal sculptor, tells of his nearly fatal encounter with a female leopard while collecting African animals for an American museum. He wounded the animal slightly with his first shot, but missed several later shots as she crossed the bed of a dry stream. Firing the last cartridge in the magazine of his rifle, he scored and the beast dropped.

But a savage snarl soon told him that the battle had not ended. Quickly reloading, he turned—to face the cat in mid-air leaping at him. She struck him in the chest, sending his weapon flying, and closed her teeth on his upper right arm. By choking her with his left hand, he was able to free his arm down to the wrist, the leopard taking successive holds with her teeth as he drew the arm inch by inch through her mouth. Then they both fell to the ground, Akeley fortunately landing on top. He succeeded in killing the animal by forcing his right fist down her throat, meanwhile choking her with his left hand and crushing her ribs with his knees. The badly mauled man staggered into camp more dead than alive. He recovered at length, and lived to utilize the mounted body of his enemy in one of the magnificent animal groups of the museum.

CHAPTER 4
More Roaring Cats

JAGUAR

The only roaring cat native to the Western Hemisphere is the jaguar. In the entire cat family only the lion and tiger are larger. From the southwestern border of the United States, the jaguar's range extends southward through Mexico and South America as far as northern Patagonia. Among Spanish-speaking people, this animal is everywhere called *el tigre,* the tiger.

In both habits and appearance it resembles the leopard, but the jaguar is larger and more heavily built. Both animals are covered with dark rosettes on a tawny background, but the rosettes of the two species differ in design. On the jaguar, the spots that form them are arranged in rough circles with one or two smaller spots in the center. The leopard's rosettes

32

Like other cats, the JAGUAR *sees well in partial darkness.
Its eyes glow by reflected light.*

are also arranged in uneven circles, but their centers are free of spots. As with leopards, completely black jaguars are not uncommon. These are chance color variants, not a different species.

Unlike most cats, jaguars seem to have no distaste for getting wet. They feed on deer, wild pigs, and other ground-living animals, and will pursue them even when they take to water. Jaguars often capture fish, turtles, and even crocodiles. This big cat is a good climber, and it sometimes catches monkeys and parrots in trees. So the jaguar's hunting grounds include land, water, and air.

An average litter contains two cubs, born after a pregnancy of about 100 days. No one knows how long jaguars may live in the wild. In captivity they have lived from fourteen to twenty years and have bred regularly. In the zoo at Rotterdam, Holland, one old veteran reached the hoary age of twenty-two years.

Jaguars vary in length from five and a half feet to nine, the long tail accounting for nearly half the overall length. Usual weights run from 125 to 250 pounds. Females are somewhat smaller than males. The largest jaguars are found in the Mato Grosso, a wild and sparsely settled section of Brazil. Here Sasha Siemel, a noted jaguar hunter, has reported killing one that weighed more than 350 pounds. Siemel's specialty is spearing jaguars single-handed. He meets an attack kneeling, holding his spear with the point toward the charging animal. The end of the shaft is braced against a rock or stuck into the ground. The onrushing cat is impaled on the spear before it can check its rush. Siemel has relieved native villages of many a notorious cattle-raider by this dangerous method.

SNOW LEOPARD

Among the handsomest of the great cats is the snow leopard, or ounce. It is classed by naturalists among the roarers, though nobody seems ever to have heard it roar.

SNOW LEOPARD

This beautiful animal is rarely seen in captivity, and little is known about its habits in its native haunts. Only a few of the cubs born in zoos have lived to become adults. The captive females that have borne cubs seem to have been poor providers. One cub, born in Leipzig, Germany, was removed from its mother and nursed by an accommodating dog for three months, but it failed to survive longer.

A male snow leopard in the Bronx Zoo of New York began life as the pet of an American pilot stationed in Burma during World War II. It was his companion on many flights "over the hump" between Burma and China. He brought it home after the war. As it grew up, it proved to be too large a pet for him to keep in a city apartment, and he turned it over to the zoo. It lived there for nearly nine years.

Lee Crandall, General Curator of the Bronx Zoo, says that this snow leopard was quite gentle, and always welcomed keepers with a purr when they visited its cage. The only difficulty they had was in ending their visits. The animal was so fond of human company that it tried to prevent the departure of a visitor by curling its body around his feet, biting and clawing his ankles. After a few such leave-takings the keepers confined their attentions to petting the animal through the bars of its cage.

Snow leopards live in the mountains of Central Asia, where they frequent high altitudes in summer. In the Himalayas, one of the members of an expedition in search of the Abominable Snowman—which they failed to find— saw a snow leopard near Mount Everest at an altitude of 14,000 feet. In winter these animals come down from the heights to live at lower altitudes. They are well protected against cold by long, heavy fur, which is gray in color with a yellowish tinge. The coat is marked with many dark spots and irregular rings.

CLOUDED LEOPARD

The clouded leopard is a slender, short-legged animal with a heavily striped and spotted gray coat. The underside of its body is nearly white. The flanks have a clouded appearance, because of large dark blotches with blackish edges, surrounded by pale areas. The bushy tail is marked with dark rings. This animal has very long canine teeth, longer in comparison with its size than those of any other modern cat. Tribesmen in Sarawak, a section of Borneo, wear them as ear ornaments.

Clouded leopards are somewhat smaller than the other great cats. The average weight for males is around 45 pounds. In the zoos of the world this species is very rare.

The habits of the clouded leopard are little known. It is described as usually living in trees, but is known to hunt on the ground at times. When hunting aloft, it preys on birds and tree-living mammals. On the ground, its favorite game is wild pig. It lives in Southeastern Asia, the Malay Peninsula, and the East Indies.

37

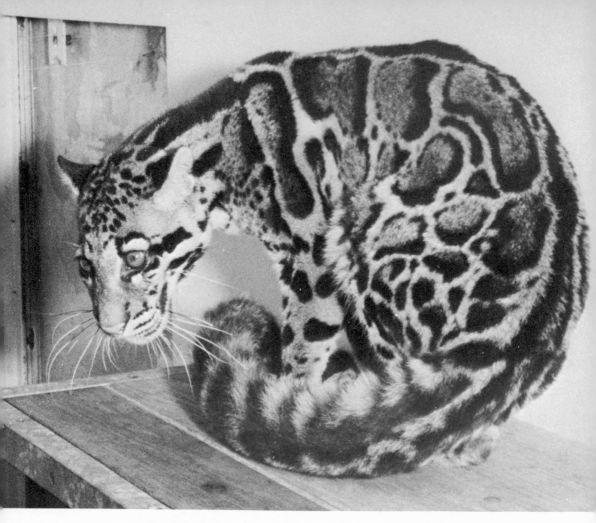

CLOUDED LEOPARD

An English hunter named Selous kept a young male of
this species as a pet in Sarawak. A fastidious feeder, it would
take no dead meat offered by its master, but would eat only
food caught by itself. Monkeys, rats, and chickens were captured by the typical cat method of stalking and pouncing.

38

Any chicken it caught was carefully plucked with its teeth before being eaten.

Selous describes the call of the clouded leopard as a moaning roar, sounding somewhat like wind blowing across the neck of an empty jug. A spray-gun, used to rid its sleeping quarters of insects, frightened it terribly.

CHEETAH

The cheetah is so different from all other cats, both in appearance and character, that it is classed as the only species in a genus of its own. About the size of a leopard, it is a taller animal, its slender body ideally built for speed. The legs are long and trim, and the feet are somewhat like the feet of a dog. The claws of other cats are long and sharp, and can be withdrawn into sheaths in the toes, as a sword is put into its scabbard. The cheetah's claws are shorter and stubbier and do not fit into sheaths. The head is relatively small and un-catlike in shape, and there is a short mane along the neck. Small, round, dark spots thickly cover the yellowish body. Very definite dark lines, running from the inside corner of each eye to the rear end of the mouth, give the face a curiously sad expression. All cats have these "tear lines," but in no other species are they so long and definite.

The cheetah is a resident of the open plains. It is not a climber, shuns the forest, and does its hunting by day. Over short distances it can run faster than any other four-footed

animal, and is said to attain speeds of sixty or even seventy miles per hour. It can overtake the swiftest antelope within a few hundred yards. No race horse or greyhound can outrun it.

Often called the hunting leopard, this cat has long been tamed and trained for sport. Its great speed, mild nature, and hunting habits make it an ideal aide for the sportsman. Instead of creeping near enough to pounce, its habit is to approach its prey stealthily to within a few hundred yards, and then run it down.

The cheetah is believed to have first been trained for hunting in Egypt, where paintings dating back to 1500 B.C. show it being led on the leash. Mongol princes of the Middle Ages kept cheetahs in large numbers. Indian nobles use

40

them today for hunting blackbuck, a very swift antelope. Their cheetahs must be imported from Africa, as this animal is now practically extinct in India and the rest of Asia.

The famous book that Marco Polo wrote about his adventurous travels in China tells how Kublai Khan, the Mongol conqueror of China, hunted with cheetahs in the thirteenth century. The cats sat behind the saddles of their mounted keepers, and jumped to the ground when game was in sight.

In India the cheetah, blindfolded, is carried to the field in a bullock cart or jeep. When game is sighted, the blindfold is removed and the animal immediately sets off in pursuit. If the first burst of speed is not successful, the cheetah gives up the chase. It cannot keep up such a swift pace over a long distance.

A young animal, captured after it has learned to hunt in the wild, is best for sport. Training requires about six months. Some cheetahs become so tame that they recognize their own names, and follow their masters like dogs. They like attention and show pleasure by purring.

A recent attempt to race cheetahs on a whippet track ended in complete failure. The contestants would not run when pitted against one another. When sent after a mechanical rabbit, they quickly caught up and tore it to pieces. When the rabbit was set to go faster than they could run, they showed complete lack of sporting blood by giving up. Matched against greyhounds, they quickly overtook the dogs and gracefully jumped over them.

CHAPTER 5

Purring Cats of the Wild

The twenty-nine species of the genus *Felis,* the "purring cats," are all wild-living with the single exception of the domestic cat. Occasionally someone attempts to make a pet of the cub of one or another of these wild animals. But when the pet grows up, it is apt to forget its early training and be given by its owner to a zoo.

A description of all these species would doubtless prove to be dull reading. In this chapter we will tell a bit about the larger purring cats and about those that are believed to have had a place in the direct ancestry of the house cat.

The various species of purring cats live in all parts of the world except Australasia, Antarctica, and Madagascar. They range in size from the puma, almost as big as a leopard, down to the little black-footed cat, slightly smaller than a house

Wild purring cats are found all over the world.
This LEOPARD CAT lives in southern Asia and the East Indies.

cat. The coats of purring cats are generally tawny yellow or gray, tending to become white on the throat, chest, and belly. In a few species, the coat is unmarked. In most, however, it is handsomely decorated with dark rosettes, spots, or stripes.

The sound that we call purring is made by the vibration of the soft palate, in the back part of the mouth. Human snoring is produced in the same way. None of these cats is ordinarily dangerous to man, though some of the larger ones may be, if cornered.

PUMA

Largest of the purring cats is the puma. Its slender, fawn-colored body is unmarked by any decoration other than black areas on the face. The puma goes by a number of other names. Among them are cougar, mountain lion, panther, and painter. Still another name, catamount, stems from the old Scottish custom of calling the European wildcat a "cat of the mountain" or "cat o' mount."

Formerly the range of this graceful animal covered most of North and South America. Pumas are still fairly common in parts of the western United States, mainly in the Rocky Mountains. On the Pacific coast, these cats range from the mountains of British Columbia down through Mexico and South America. The only ones now found in the eastern United States live in Florida and Louisiana. Occasionally a hunter reports hearing a "painter" scream in the woods of Maine or some other eastern state. Usually it turns out that he has only heard a bobcat's caterwauling.

Puma cubs are perhaps the most playful of all young cats. They seem never to tire of mock battles, wrestling, rolling, and jumping over one another. Adults retain their cub-like ways to some extent, and a mother sometimes joins in the rough play of her offspring. At birth cubs have dark spots over their bodies and black rings around their tails. These soon disappear, though they can still be seen in some adults. Litters contain from two to four kittens, born after a pregnancy of about 95 days.

The Indians of Peru gave the name puma to this animal long before the Spaniards conquered the Inca kingdom. These Indians depended on their herds of guanacos and vicuñas for both meat to eat and wool for clothing. Pumas made tremendous inroads on the herds, killing many of the young animals shortly after birth. To protect the young ones, the Incas organized great drives on the predators at the time of year when the domestic herds were breeding. Thousands of Indians would form a great circle, surrounding an area perhaps ten miles in diameter. Slowly advancing, the men drove the pumas to a central spot where they were slaughtered with spears.

Ranch owners have always been bitter foes of the puma, for it is a great killer of young cattle, sheep, and horses. Breeders run down the big cats with dogs, catch them in

traps, or poison them. That the species has not been wiped out long ago speaks well for its ability to avoid enemies.

Most naturalists agree that the rancher's prejudice against the puma is not entirely justified. It is true that this cat, if it lives in ranching country, preys to some extent on domestic stock. But so important a species of our wildlife heritage should not be wiped out because of the loss of a few colts and calves.

Pumas as a rule do not live in ranching country, but keep to wild, unsettled localities, where their prey consists largely of deer. The deer, unless kept within bounds by natural predators, are likely to become too numerous to be supported by the available forage. When this occurs, many deer starve. So in the long run, the puma's raids are a benefit to the deer herds.

LYNX

In cold northern forests, the lynx leaves its great paw marks in the snow as it trails the snowshoe rabbit. Anyone lucky enough to catch sight of this furtive hunter will be astonished to find that an animal weighing only twenty or thirty pounds can make such huge tracks. Its big feet, bordered in winter with long, stiff hairs, act as snowshoes, enabling it to travel through deep snow without floundering.

This cat's thick fur marks it as an inhabitant of cold countries. The Canada lynx is common in most of Canada

47

A PUMA *treed by dogs.*

The broad feet of the CANADIAN LYNX *serve as snowshoes.*

and Alaska. A few are still found in the United States south
of the Canadian border. An occasional lynx turns up in
northern New England, the Adirondack Mountains of New
York, and farther west along the shores of the Great Lakes.
A very close relative ranges across northern Europe and
Asia.

The stocky body of the lynx is kept warm by a handsome
coat decorated with patches of tawny yellow, dark brown,
and cinnamon. Its face is framed in a luxurious set of side-
burns and chin whiskers, which are marked with black
stripes. The pointed ears end in tufts of stiff, black hairs,

and the stubby tail has a black tip.

The favorite prey of the lynx is the snowshoe rabbit. In the far north, a fatal disease attacks these rabbits every few years, and they die by thousands. At such times, trappers take very few lynx pelts compared with the number they take when rabbits are plentiful. The cats, deprived of their favorite food supply, grow thin and hungry. Trappers on Alaska's Mount McKinley say that many lynxes starve when the rabbits disappear, rather than change their diet to some other animal which may be plentiful.

In less rigorous climates, lynxes are not so choosy. Lemmings, squirrels, and mice—as well as foxes, wild sheep, and fawns—are all on the bill of fare.

BOBCAT

A smaller relative of the Canada lynx is the American wildcat. Called also bobcat, because of its short tail, and bay lynx, from its bay color, it lives in Southern Canada and throughout the United States and Mexico. A big bobcat may be heavier than a small lynx, but on the average the bobcat is a somewhat smaller animal.

Aside from its stump of a tail, a bobcat might be taken for a large house cat. But no one who knows it well would ever try to make a pet of it, for it is a spitting, snarling ball of fury when aroused. In a fight or during mating season, its wild music outdoes that of any city tomcat.

49

Though the bobcat sometimes lives in forests near towns, it is seldom seen. It knows very well how to keep itself hidden during the day, and hunts only at night. Farmers are relentless enemies of this cat, for it raids their chicken coops and preys on other barnyard fowl, as well as lambs and calves. Hunters pursue it with dogs, and it will flee before a baying pack of hounds. But if they corner it, a tremendous fight is in store. Many a hound has limped from such a battle licking its wounds.

The color of the bobcat varies greatly in different parts of its range. Generally, the coat is reddish brown above, shading to white on the chest and belly. Dark streaks and spots overlie the ground color. The tail is marked with indistinct rings, and the tip is black on top and white underneath. This distinguishes it from the lynx's tail, which has a black tip both above and below. The ears end in tufts of long black hair.

Forests, swamps, deserts, and mountains seem to be equally acceptable as homes for these small cats. They usually hunt on the ground, but can climb well, and catch roosting birds in the trees. On the ground, they prey on rabbits and other small animals. The bobcat has mastered the art of capturing porcupines without getting its hide full of quills. It manages this by attacking the under parts of a porky, where quills do not grow.

Bobcats mate with house cats occasionally, but the kittens born of such crossbreeding seldom if ever survive.

BOBCAT *(American wildcat)*

OCELOT

A few years ago a young ocelot that had been captured in Panama when a cub, and raised as a pet, was brought to New York. Its owner, who lived in the city, soon found that it was "too much cat" to keep in his small quarters. So he gave it to a friend who had a large place in the country. The new owner, a man of some experience with wild animals, led it on a leash through the streets to his suburban train, and got it to his home without difficulty. It soon fitted into the life of the family, and showed every evidence of tameness and good will. The children grew very fond of the beautiful young animal, and it played with them by the hour.

One evening some weeks later, the father came home from work to find his terrified family locked in the kitchen. The ocelot was in full possession of the rest of the house. It had suddenly gone wild, showing such ferocity that the mother hastily gathered her children and fled into the kitchen.

The father armed himself with a heavy overcoat and went on a room-to-room search. He finally found the ocelot on top of a bookcase in the living room. As it jumped to the floor, he fell on the snarling cat and wrapped the overcoat tightly around its body. After a struggle, he managed to snap a leash on its collar and confine its legs so the sharp claws could not tear him. Next day, he found a home for it in a zoo.

Many attempts have been made to tame the ocelot, for it is one of the most graceful and beautiful of all the small

The beautiful OCELOT

cats. Its mild disposition and ready response to kindly treatment would seem to qualify it as an ideal pet. But too many of these pets have gone wild to justify anyone in saying that this is a safe animal to have around the house.

The ocelot lives in tropical and subtropical American forests. Its home extends from the southwestern border of the United States down to northern Argentina. The yellowish coat is boldly striped with black on the head and neck. Black spots on the feet and legs grow on the body into large black-bordered ovals with brown centers. These handsome markings form chains along the back and sides.

Prey consists largely of birds and monkeys. Pairs are believed to stay together for life. The cubs, usually two to a litter, are born in rocky dens or hollow logs.

KAFFIR CAT

Living in various parts of the world are three species of small purring cats which are important because they are believed to have had a part in the house cat's origin. These three species are the Kaffir cat (or African wildcat), the jungle cat, and the European wildcat. Only brief descriptions will be given here. Their connection with the domestic cat will be shown later.

Kaffir cats, with a weight of about eight pounds, are only a little heavier and larger than the average house cat. The head and body are decorated with rather thin stripes, somewhat like tabby markings. The tail is ringed with dark stripes, and ends in a black patch. The legs and feet also are usually black. Lying hidden by day, this cat comes out at night to hunt small mammals and birds. Its range covers most of Africa, except the large deserts and rain forests. It also lives in the islands of the Mediterranean Sea and in parts of Asia. This species interbreeds freely with house cats.

KAFFIR CAT *(African wildcat)*

JUNGLE CAT

In Burma, India, and westward to the Mediterranean lives the jungle cat. A considerably larger animal than the Kaffir cat, it sometimes weighs as much as twenty pounds. The color is gray or tawny, overlaid with a darker tabby pattern. The ears have short tufts at the tips, and the tail is marked with dark rings.

JUNGLE CAT

EUROPEAN WILDCAT

The European wildcat is the best known among the few cat species that still live on that continent. Its continued presence in such a thickly populated part of the world proves that it is adept at taking care of itself. Living in forests across Europe and into Asia Minor, it is now rare everywhere except in northern Scotland. There it is fairly common, and has

EUROPEAN *(Scottish)* WILDCAT

come to be known as the Scottish wildcat for that reason.

In the highlands of Scotland, it seems to be increasing in numbers. Some owners of hunting estates protect it, in spite of its raids on their rabbits, grouse, and other game. The great wars of the twentieth century, when most young High- landers were away with the armed forces, seem to have benefited the Scottish wildcat—perhaps the only benefit that can be granted those two world disasters. The absence of so many men brought about a truce in the battle that Scots have always waged against these raiders of their sheepfolds and barnyards.

By nature savage and untamable, this animal is one of the fiercest predators in Europe. Slightly larger than a house cat, it has striped markings similar to those of many domestic tabby cats. The legs are long, and the thickly furred tail ends in a bushy black tip.

In mating season, the European wildcat sounds off with unearthly caterwaulings. In Scotland, the female often bears two litters a year. Usually there are two cubs to a litter. When opportunity offers, this species will mate with domestic cats. Such a mating is usually between a domestic female and a wild tom. The crossbred offspring never make lovable pets. They do not take to domestic life, and almost always join their wild kinfolk after weaning. For this reason, many of the Scottish wildcats are now of mixed blood.

58

CHAPTER 6

From Wild Animal to Household Pet

Early man tamed animals that could be useful to him. Horses, camels, cattle, sheep, dogs, swine, fowls: all are helpful, each in its own way, in the daily life of the human race. These animals work for us, help us hunt, or give their lives to provide our food.

Then why did men in later times tame the cat? This animal is neither a source of food nor a beast of burden. Except for the cheetah and the caracal, no cat can be trained to assist human hunters. Its only practical use is as a destroyer of rats, mice, and other rodents. This may have been the reason why people first brought cats into their homes, although it is hardly a primary reason for keeping them today.

Cats were not tamed till long after other wild creatures had become close associates of man. Some observers believe that cats have never become as thoroughly tamed as our other domestic animals. With the occasional exception of the horse, the others have long since lost the ability to be completely self-supporting, and are largely dependent on their masters. Cats, wherever they have access to the outdoors, can and do make their own living. Even in cities, where there are no woods and fields, alley cats do very well for themselves. Treasured house pets sometimes take to the fields permanently, seeming to prefer the wild life of their ancestors to a life of luxurious ease.

Cats are the only animals that accept the comforts provided by man without submitting to his dominance. They do not depend on us. They merely accept us. They certainly show affection at times, but their affection is bestowed strictly on their own terms. They are not "back slappers." We must conclude that most of us keep cats because they are beautiful and graceful creatures that we enjoy having around us. Many people prefer their dignified reserve, often amounting to indifference, to the unquestioning obedience and adoration of a dog.

Your cat does not always come running when you call it. If it happens to be in the mood, it will jump into your lap for a bit of attention, and show its satisfaction by contented purring. But when the mood passes, it jumps to the floor and walks away without so much as "by your leave." Cats really own their masters, rather than their masters' owning them. In spite of these qualities—or perhaps because of them—cats are today the most numerous of all pets.

A cat may not come when you call.

No one knows surely just where, when, and why men were first prompted to welcome cats as house guests. As to where and when, we have some evidence. As to why, we can only guess.

Statuettes of cats have been found in Egyptian graves dating from 2600 B.C. Since they prove that the Egyptians had tame cats at that time, domestication must have occurred earlier, probably much earlier. But at least these statuettes show that cats were kept as pets in Egyptian homes more than 4500 years ago. No evidence of a domesticated cat appears in the record of any other country until long after that time.

As old as these Egyptian records are, they are recent compared with the history of other domestic animals. The bones of dogs have been found in the campsites of men who lived at least 10,000 years ago, and the association of man and dog doubtless goes back much farther than that. No evidence that the cave man kept cats has ever been discovered. So as far as European domestic cats are concerned, the "where" was probably ancient Egypt. The domestic cats of Asia appear to have had different forebears, as we shall see.

As to why cats were domesticated by man, we can only hazard a reasonable guess.

The yearly overflow of the River Nile leaves a deposit of rich soil when it recedes. In this fertile strip along both sides of the great river, the ancient Egyptians raised crops of grain which they stored in granaries for use as needed.

Because the rest of Egypt was desert country where no grain could be grown, the bread of the people depended on the stored grain. Its protection against the inroads of rats and mice was of prime importance to the nation's well-being.

In the country along the Nile valley lived a small cat described in the previous chapter, the Kaffir cat or African wildcat. What could be more reasonable than to suppose that Egyptian farmers welcomed at their granaries these natural enemies of rats and mice? In time, the cats would begin to sense that they could take advantage of this rich hunting ground without danger. They would gradually grow tamer and begin to hunt inside houses, where they would find themselves equally welcome. Eventually, they would come to be unafraid in the presence of men and take their place as permanent inmates of the household. There is no proof for all this, but it is surely a reasonable explanation as to how the cat came to be a domestic animal. How it later flourished in Egypt, and increased greatly in dignity and importance, will be the subject of the next chapter.

The domesticated Egyptian cat was probably carried to the countries bordering the Mediterranean Sea in the ships of Phoenician traders. These adventurous people were the merchant mariners of the ancient world. Their principal home ports were the cities of Tyre and Sidon, on the eastern shore of the Mediterranean. In their seagoing vessels, they carried rich cargoes of trade goods all through the great inland sea, exchanging their wares for slaves, metals, or whatever they could sell at a profit at home. Sailing through the Strait of Gibraltar, known to the ancients as the Pillars of Hercules, they brought jewelry, cloth, and other products of the civilized East to barter with the rude tribes that lived along the coasts of Europe. The Phoenicians may have traded with the people of the British Isles, and there is some evidence that they reached the Scandinavian countries.

An occasional cat must have joined a Phoenician ship when it docked in Egypt. Practically every ship has a few cats on the free passenger list. They walk aboard from the docks and make themselves at home. Often welcomed as killers of cargo-destroying rats, they are not hustled ashore as a human stowaway would be.

Some of these cat stowaways doubtless went ashore at ports visited later during the voyage. No matter where an Egyptian cat "jumped ship," it would always find plenty of its own kin to make it feel at home. The European wildcat was then common all over its home continent. These animals mated with the domesticated Egyptian cats. Some of these crossbreeds, perhaps influenced by their domestic ancestry, took up their traditional work as mousers in the homesteads of the local inhabitants.

The cats brought to Italy by Phoenician traders prospered in their new surroundings. By the beginning of the Christian Era, they were welcome in many Roman households. From Rome, they spread throughout the Empire, and mated with native wildcats to form a mixed breed.

Thousands of years ago, cats probably stowed away on ships just as this modern cat is doing.

In the first century A.D. the Roman legions conquered Britain. They found no tame cats there, but plenty of wild ones. For four hundred years, what is now England and Wales was ruled by the conquerors. Many Roman families settled permanently in Britain, bringing their cats along with them. At the sites of some of their villas, remains of cats have been found. As on the continent, these house cats doubtless mated with the local European wildcats.

In Wales cats were present in the tenth century, but they were evidently rare, for their price was fixed by law. A Welsh prince of that time, called Howel the Good, decreed laws establishing the value of cats of various ages and talents. A newborn kitten was priced at one penny. When it had proved its usefulness by catching a mouse, it was worth two-pence. One that had won an outstanding reputation as a mouser sold at fourpence. If a man killed another man's cat, he was obliged to pay damages to the owner, the amount of which was determined in a novel way. The body of the animal was hung by the tip of its tail so that its nose just touched a smooth barn floor. Then grain, furnished by the offender, was poured over the suspended corpse till the heap rose to the end of the tail. In this way, the owner was repaid for the grain that would be eaten by mice because of the loss of his mouser.

Very little is known about the origin of the domestic cats of Asia. The breeds differ one from another in various parts of that continent, just as they do in other continents. But the differences are largely skin-deep. The basic anatomy of all cats is much the same, no matter where they live.

Many of the Asiatic cats are more slender and lanky than our breeds, and the legs are longer. The ears of some breeds are narrow and pointed, and the eyes of many have a downward slant. In the countries of southeastern Asia, cats often have kinky tails, such as we see occasionally in our Siamese cats. No one can account for this peculiarity, but a Maylayan folk tale makes an ingenious attempt. According to this legend a certain princess, bathing in a lake on the palace grounds, strung her rings and bracelets for safekeeping on the tail of her pet cat. While she was in the water, the pet switched its tail and all the jewelry flew off into the lake and was lost. The next time the princess went for a swim, she was equipped with new adornments. Again she strung her baubles on the pet's tail, but tied a knot in it so they would not slide off. Since then, Malayan cats have had kinky tails. A likely story!

In India, the jungle cat, mentioned in the preceding chapter, may have been tamed long ago to found a race of house cats. References to domestic cats occur in Indian literature of some 2000 years ago.

Moslems have always been kind to cats, following the example of their prophet Mohammed, who was greatly attached to his cat Muezza. One day, Mohammed was called on an important errand while Muezza lay asleep on the outstretched sleeve of his robe. Rather than awaken her, he

Domestic cats, such as this SIAMESE, *have long been known in the Far East.*

cut off the sleeve and went on his errand, leaving his pet to finish her nap undisturbed.

Domestic cats have long been known in China, Japan, and other eastern Asiatic countries. Confucius, the father of Chinese culture, owned one in the fourth century B.C., and cats were kept in Japanese temples from very early times. The Siamese cat, while nothing is known of its origin, has long been a popular pet in its home country. Some of the cats kept in Siamese temples were held sacred, because they were marked with two dark patches on the shoulders. These were said to be spots left by a god, who had once picked up a cat and left the shadow of his hand forever on its descendants.

What wild species, or crossbreeding of tamed species,

produced the different types of Asiatic house cats is not known. But it is evident that their direct ancestry is different from that of our cats. They are believed to be descendants of several species of Asiatic wildcats.

Early European explorers found plenty of dogs, but no tame cats, in the villages of American Indians. The first house cats in the New World doubtless came as free passengers in the ships of early settlers. Whether there were any on the vessels of Columbus, or of later explorers, is not recorded. It is likely that the *Mayflower* passengers, who came to stay permanently, brought their cats along with their household goods.

From all this speculation about origins, at least one fact is fairly well established: the world's domestic cats, as we know them, are the result of the taming, in ages past, of various kinds of wild cats. Our pets are a mixture of several species. To be exact, they are not really a *species* at all. They are a *breed,* but a breed of such long standing that it has been raised by naturalists to the dignity of a species.

A great Swedish scientist of the eighteenth century, Carl Linnaeus, originated the system of scientific naming that we still follow. He lived more than two hundred years ago, and did not know as much about the history of cats as is known today. He considered the domestic cat a true species, and named it *Felis catus*. Scientists still follow Linnaeus' usage and recognize our house pet as a species.

CHAPTER 7
An Egyptian God

In the religion of ancient Egypt, many of the gods were identified with certain animals, such as the hawk, jackal, bull, or lion. Statues of these gods, like that of Pasht described in Chapter 1, represented them as men or women. But the heads were those of the animals with which they were identified.

The animal that appears most prominently in Egyptian mythology is the cat. It was closely identified with both Ra, the sun god, and Pasht, the moon goddess. The Egyptian word *mau* or *meau* had two meanings, sun and cat. Pronounce it aloud and you will realize that it sounds like the most usual sound that a cat makes.

In the cat, the Egyptians saw many of the qualities that were ascribed to Pasht. This was her particular animal, and she was shown in sculptures and paintings as a woman with

---

The Egyptian goddess Pasht was represented as a woman with a cat's head.

a cat's head. Pasht was the consort and closest companion of Ra, whose passage across the sky made the light of day. Every evening at sundown, he disappeared into the underworld, and darkness enveloped the earth.

During the night Pasht, as the moon, held the sun's rays in her glowing cat's eyes and helped Ra find his way through the gloom of the underworld. On every one of these journeys his passage was opposed by Apap, the monstrous serpent of darkness, whom he must fight and conquer before he could leave the underworld to bring on another day. Ra assumed the form of a cat to fight these battles, which he invariably won, leaving Apap torn and bleeding. But always on the next nightly round, Ra found the serpent completely restored to health and spoiling for another fight.

For many of her activities, Pasht actually changed herself into a cat, so it was quite possible that any stray puss might be the goddess herself. The people firmly believed these myths, and looked upon every cat as a sacred animal.

The laws of Egypt strictly forbade the removal of a cat from the country, and any Egyptian traveler who found one in a foreign land was expected to bring it back home. It was a capital offense to cause the death of a cat, even by accident.

Herodotus, an early Greek traveler in Egypt, has left us a record of his experiences, in which appear many incidents showing the importance of the sacred animal. He says it was a greater crime to kill a cat than to murder a man. In case a house caught fire, the first concern of the fire fighters was to rescue the cats; only after this had been done were attempts made to save the occupants and their property. Herodotus thought there were entirely too many cats in Egypt. If cats were then as tireless breeders of kittens as they are now, we would probably have agreed with him. They must have swarmed in homes, streets, palaces, and temples.

Because cats were believed to protect a household from misfortune, every family kept them. When a house cat died, the family went into deep mourning, expressing sorrow by shaving off their eyebrows. The mummified body of the pet, placed in an elaborate mummy case, was buried with solemn rites in a cat cemetery. One of these special burying grounds was near every temple. Just as a human mummy was supplied with food for use in the afterworld, so was a cat's mummy supplied with bowls of milk—and even mummified mice. In one of these graveyards, excavated not many years ago, literally tons of cat mummies were unearthed. A whole shipload of them was taken to England and sold for making fertilizer.

If a wealthy Egyptian family lost its cat, the mummy was wrapped in fine linen of two colors, wound in elaborate patterns. The mummy case, often made of bronze and decorated with jewels, was taken to the great cat cemetery of the temple of Pasht at Bubastis. This city was especially devoted to the worship of the cat-headed goddess, and here was her principal temple, a magnificent structure of red granite. In its inner shrine was the huge statue of the goddess.

Cat mummies from ancient Egypt.

Priests reverently attended the many cats that were kept in the shrine, where they slept on soft cushions, ate dainty food, and were buried in especially ornate mummy cases.

One of the principal religious festivals of the Egyptians was celebrated at Bubastis in honor of Pasht. Herodotus says that some 700,000 people attended this celebration every spring. It was a festive occasion, accompanied by feasting, music, and dancing.

An eclipse of the sun was conceived by these imaginative

people to be a titanic battle to the death between Ra and Apap, the powers of light and darkness. For such a struggle, Ra took the form of a giant cat. If he should fail to triumph over Apap, there would be no more daylight, so the people watched an eclipse with breathless anxiety. As they observed the gradual disappearance of the sun, they set up a great clamor and shouted at the top of their lungs in an attempt to distract Apap's attention from the fight. When the sun again appeared, as it always did, they knew the cat had won, and great rejoicing took the place of terror.

After an eclipse, the reverence and devotion in which the cat was held mounted to its highest pitch. At one such time, when a Roman soldier at Alexandria was so ill advised as to kill a cat, an outraged mob fell upon him and served him as he had served his victim.

Early in the fourth century B.C. a Persian king, attacking the Egyptian city of Memphis, found it so heavily fortified that his army was unable to conquer it after many assaults. Then he resorted to extremely novel tactics. The Persians had no reverence for the gods of their enemies, but had some knowledge of the Egyptian religion. Collecting several hundred cats, they hurled them over the walls into the city. The defenders were so horrified at this blasphemous treatment of the sacred animals that they had little power to resist. The attack that followed the cat bombardment caused the surrender of the city.

Egyptian cats were graceful animals, slim and lithe, with

pointed ears and rather long legs. They usually wore dark tabby markings on a ginger-colored background. We can be quite sure of their appearance, for a great many cat statuettes have been found in tombs and the ruins of temples. Cat ornaments and charms were widely popular, made in various sizes of all materials from gold to baked clay. Body markings were sometimes indicated by insets of colored stone. The most usual form of statuette showed the animal sitting on its haunches, the front feet resting on the ground, and the body, head and ears erect.

This is by no means the only posture shown in Egyptian statuettes. Both in paintings and in sculptures, cats are shown sitting under chairs, nursing kittens, and engaging in many other forms of cat activity.

A painting now in the British Museum shows a cat retrieving wounded waterfowl from a lotus swamp, as its master stands nearby in his boat. This picture would seem to indicate that the Egyptians trained their cats to help them hunt. No modern hunter has been able to do such a thing. Domestic cats are instinctive hunters, to be sure, but their hunting is strictly for their own benefit, not to assist a master. It is almost impossible to teach them to do anything that they do not want to do, and certainly most cats do not want to go into water. However, fishing cats, even swimming cats, are not entirely unknown. Perhaps the Egyptian artist simply imagined this hunting scene, and did not intend to show an incident that he had actually observed.

An Egyptian cat helps its master hunt.
The cat is to the left of the man, under his elbow.

CHAPTER 8

From God to Demon

The leadership of Egypt in the ancient world gradually declined under the onslaughts of foreign invaders. A final blow by the Roman legions in 58 B.C. crushed Egypt's power.

The gods of Egypt fell along with the empire, though some of them, under different names, found a place in the mythology of the conquerors. Early in the fourth century A.D. during the reign of Constantine, the Roman Empire adopted the Christian religion. With the gradual spread of Christianity throughout the Roman world, the gods of the old religion became the demons of the new. The leaders of the early Church made every effort to debase the pagan gods, and encouraged any ideas that would discourage their worship.

Pasht, the moon goddess, was identified in Roman mythology with the goddess Diana, who was thought to have three distinct forms. As Diana, her province was the earth; as Luna,

A Roman cat in the Colosseum.

she was goddess of the moon; and as Hecate, she presided over witchcraft and sorcery in the underworld. The evil companions of Hecate, witches and wizards, accompanied her on frequent spell-casting visits to the earth. On these excursions Hecate, as well as her companions, often assumed the form of a cat. Even the ruler of the underworld at times transformed himself into a black cat. In Egyptian mythology, the companions of Pasht had been cats, so the companions of Hecate, her successor in the newer mythology, were likewise cats. And this association of cats with the underworld was continued in Christian thought.

This was indeed a far cry from the honor and reverence that had been accorded the sacred animal of the cat goddess.

Belief in the partnership of cats and witches has long had a place in the folklore of many countries. This superstition may well be a survival of the fear in which the saber-toothed tiger was held, as the most dreaded of all the enemies of prehistoric man. Whatever its origin, the idea that cats are in league with the powers of darkness and evil has persisted even into our own times.

So cats came to be looked upon as demons by the early Christians, and to be feared as the animal whose form demons most often assumed. This widespread belief made the centuries following the fall of Rome, now known as the Dark Ages, a sad time for cats. Far from being worshiped, they came to be hated and persecuted unmercifully.

In those times a black curtain of superstition spread over the western world and shut out the light of learning. Men forgot their skills and arts, and much of the progress of civilization came to a halt. Only monks in secluded monasteries continued, in some measure, to keep the light of knowledge burning.

From king to peasant, few people doubted the existence of witches and wizards, women and men who had sold themselves to the devil. The common belief was that, as servants of Satan, they devoted their lives to carrying out his evil plots against the well-being of mankind. In return, Satan was supposed to have conferred on them mystical powers, chiefly the ability to bring misfortune, sickness, and death to all whom they chose to harm. Satan was the god they were thought to worship. They were held to be bitter enemies of the Church, and to aim their every act at its destruction. It is no wonder that devout people who credited such myths considered it their duty to destroy the wicked enemies of all they held most sacred. And cats, the friends and helpers of witches and wizards, shared equally in the persecution of their masters.

Many less harmful superstitions about cats persist to this day. Who has not felt a slight uneasiness if a black cat happened to cross his path? Cats are supposed to be omens of both good and bad luck. Many sailors believe a calico cat can predict the coming of a storm. If a cat sneezes in the presence of the bride on her wedding day, the marriage will supposedly be a happy one. If a cat sits with its tail to the fire, some people believe there will soon be rain. On Halloween, cats and witches are said to fly about on broomsticks.

Dozens of proverbs and wise sayings have their origin in the instinctive behavior of cats. "When the cat is away the mice will play." "A cat with a straw tail sitteth not before the fire." "Honest as a cat when the meat is out of reach." "Fain would the cat eat fish, but she is loath to wet her feet." There are many more examples.

Superstitious people have always imagined mysterious traits in this self-contained animal. Cats' eyes shine at night and they see very well in partial darkness. The eyes shine because there is a membrane behind the retina which reflects light. Cats see in the dark because their pupils open wider as the light grows dimmer. But these natural explanations were not understood. Early man feared the dark, and the cat's ability to go about confidently at night seemed to prove that it was in league with the supernatural. Cats walk noiselessly on padded feet, suggesting stealth and slyness. While sitting quietly looking at nothing, a cat will sometimes start violently, as if it had suddenly seen something invisible to human eyes. All these traits, and many others, have built up the cat's reputation as a creature of mystery.

But the superstition that has brought most suffering to cats is their supposed connection with the practice of witchcraft. In medieval times, and even in later centuries, it

was believed that every witch owned a cat. This was her crony, the sharer in her evil schemes, her means of transportation, and the form which she frequently assumed. Old women were those most often accused of the crime of witchcraft. The penalty for anyone found guilty was death. Judges and witnesses were usually convinced before trial of the guilt of the accused, and their efforts were mainly directed toward forcing a confession, often by means of torture. Aged women, and strong men too, would confess almost anything to gain relief from the pain of the rack and thumbscrew.

In the hope of diverting blame from themselves, alleged witches on trial often accused others of taking part in their

Three Englishwomen, convicted of witchcraft in the seventeenth century, shown with their cat and other animal helpers.

wicked practices. And they usually put part or all of the blame on their cats. If the defendant was found guilty, her cat was likewise guilty, and was obliged to suffer punishment along with her.

In the old court records, there are many accounts of witch trials. The evidence presented was often so incredible that it is difficult for us today to understand how any judge could accept it as proof of guilt. But we should remember that most men, high and low, had complete faith in the evil power of witches, and were only too willing to believe any hearsay evidence against them.

There were men who made it their sole business to discover witches and bring them to trial. These professional witch hunters brought thousands of innocent people to their deaths. Because they received a fixed sum for each witch they denounced, they were not over-scrupulous as to evidence before accusing a suspect.

Superstitious belief in witches long outlived the Dark Ages. One evening in 1618, two old English women were sitting at tea in their kitchen, when their hungry cat Rutterkin begged a share of the food. One of them waved her kerchief at the pet to make it go away. This innocent gesture brought about the conviction and execution of the two women when later they were tried for causing the death by witchcraft of the Earl of Rutland's children. Waving the kerchief was held by the court to prove that the accused communicated mysteriously with devils. Thousands of men and women were put to death during the sixteenth and seventeenth centuries on such flimsy evidence. And their cats usually shared the same fate.

King James VI of Scotland, who became James I of England in 1603, was a confirmed witch hunter. As a young man, he married a princess of Denmark. While sailing home with his bride, his fleet ran into a great storm off the coast of Scotland. The king was convinced that Satan, working through local witches, had made an effort to drown him, and ordered that the guilty assistants be found and punished.

Doctor John Fian, an alleged sorcerer, was accused of being one of Satan's helpmates in this attempted treason. A witness testified that Fian "had been seen to chase a cat high above the ground with great swiftness and as lightly as the cat herself." When questioned, Dr. Fian testified that Satan, at a great assemblage of witches, had ordered them all to go through certain magical rites with their cats, then to cast them into the sea. The purpose of this was to "raise winds for the destruction of ships and boats." Though Fian insisted that he had refused to obey Satan's orders, he was convicted and executed.

Another of Satan's suspected assistants in the same treasonable plot was Agnes Sampson, a reputed witch. After suffering torture, she confessed that she and two hundred of her evil companions had sailed out to sea in sieves (a favorite vessel of witches) and had thrown their cats overboard off the town of Leith, directly in the course of the king's fleet.

"This," she said, "caused such a tempest as a greater hath not been seen." The ship carrying His Majesty caught the worst of the contrary wind, was separated from the other vessels of the fleet, and barely escaped going on the rocks. Dame Sampson testified further that the king "would never have come safely from the sea if his faith had not prevailed over our intentions."

King James was able to confirm in every detail Agnes Sampson's testimony as to the danger in which his ship had been placed by the storm. After this experience, he proved a tireless enemy of witches during all the rest of his reign. Among his many assaults on witchcraft was a book in which he urged his subjects to be ever on the alert to seek out witches and bring them to justice.

Many weird cat stories have a place in the folklore of Europe. One of the most famous concerns a traveler who is walking along a lonely forest path at night. He meets a troop of cats carrying a small coffin on top of which rests a tiny jeweled crown. Horrified by this strange funeral procession, the man runs through the forest to a nearby village and takes refuge in a lighted cottage. As he tells his story, the family cat, lying asleep on the hearth, suddenly leaps into the fire shrieking, "Then I am king of the cats!" As it scrambles up the chimney, it cries, "I am on my way to claim the crown!"

The evil superstitions that destroyed so many innocent people have gradually given way to more reasonable thought.

Men, women, and cats are no longer tried and condemned as witches. Old customs that involved the sacrifice of cats during Lent, Easter, and certain holidays have long since fallen into disfavor. Until some three hundred years ago, an annual bonfire at midsummer in Paris was fed with wicker cages full of cats. Happily, such celebrations are things of the past.

But superstitions harmful to cats still persist here and there. It was long a custom in farming districts of France to kill a cat to celebrate the end of harvest season. This sacrifice to the corn god is believed to occur even now in some rural neighborhoods. But whatever cat superstitions still linger are mostly innocent and harmless, having to do with good luck or bad, foretelling rain, and the like.

The lot of our feline friends has changed very much for the better. There has been no change in the character of cats, but there has been a change in the hearts of men toward their fellow creatures. In England, the scene of so many witch trials, cats had become treasured pets in some homes as long ago as the sixteenth century, when Erasmus, the great Dutch scholar, visited there. He wrote a friend that when he called on an English family, he was expected to kiss all members of the household, not omitting the cat. Doubtless such extreme politeness is no longer expected, but cats are nevertheless held in high esteem in most English homes, as in those of America and many other countries.

MAINE COON CAT

Cats are still welcome on farms.

CHAPTER 9

Better Days for Domestic Cats

In our day, cats have become much more than mere catchers of mice. The number owned purely as pets far exceeds those kept primarily as mousers. It is still true that no farmer would want to be without cats around his barns. Grocery stores, butcher shops, and restaurants still keep cats to discourage free-loading rats and mice, but cats are no longer the only means of controlling the rodent population. Better mousetraps have been invented. Corncribs are built to be rodent-proof, and houses, particularly in cities, have rat-proof cellars and walls. Modern packaging protects food sold in grocery stores from the raids of non-paying customers. All these improvements have greatly affected the cat's hunting activities. Mouse catching has become pussy's favorite sport, rather than her regular business.

Most cats are now treasured as decorative and entertaining

companions. They do not have to work for a living, spend much of their time asleep by the fire, and accept food and lodging as their due. These charming house guests repay their hosts in many ways, but not by working for them. They are comfortably housed, and their diet is carefully planned. If they are sick, skilled doctors are called in to treat them. They have indeed come upon better days.

Though life on the whole goes very well for cats in our times, we do not mean to suggest that all of them live in luxury. In every great city hordes of homeless cats roam back yards by night, fighting terrific battles in the alleys, and awakening sleepers with their wild yowlings among the chimney pots. Many alley cats are born of homeless parents, remain homeless vagabonds through life, and beget many litters of vagabond kittens. They know no other existence, and seem to be content with their lot.

Most of these carefree nomads get along rather well, too. Mice and rats are still to be found, especially around docks and warehouses. Garbage cans often offer rich pickings. Gutters may be cluttered with choice morsels, dropped by careless passers-by. Many strays are fed by kindly ladies, who run regular feeding stations in places that their boarders know well.

An alley cat leads a precarious life, with automobiles as perhaps the chief hazard. If a car makes a thorough job of it, the victim is lucky. If it is only injured, one of our 500 humane societies will care for it, or if necessary, put it pain-

Alley cats find food in garbage cans.

lessly out of its misery. These merciful organizations make a practice of gathering up old and sick alley cats, or those injured in accidents and street battles. Some humane societies run adoption services and, when possible, find new homes for foundlings.

People who live in city apartments often find it difficult to dispose of surplus cats and kittens. The best way to solve this problem is to ask a humane society to take over. But some people solve it by taking their unwanted cats to the country to abandon them by the roadside. A good proportion of these foundlings survive this rugged test of their ability to fend for themselves. Almost any countryside near a city has its quota of deserted cats roaming the fields in search of food. They live on rabbits, field mice, and other small rodents, and sleep in barns and haymows. Usually these vagabonds are fat and sleek, showing that they have learned to live very comfortably under conditions entirely different from their former ones.

Now and then an exile from the city takes up permanent quarters in a hayloft, or makes friends with a child in the fields and follows it home. If made to feel welcome, the stray may adopt the family and return to a sheltered way of life. But the majority seem to like their freedom, and remain life-long nomads.

In 1958 a can manufacturing company wished to estimate how many tin cans they might sell to makers of prepared cat food. Their survey placed the feline population at around 27 million. *Cats,* a magazine published for fanciers and breeders, estimates that there are some 32 million cats now living in the United States.

The Cat Fanciers' Association, largest of several organizations of cat owners and breeders, registers more than ten thousand animals every year. Some 150 cat clubs are members of this country-wide group, and about 200 more clubs belong to five other cat organizations. Most of the registered cats are blue bloods, those that have pedigrees and compete for prizes in cat shows. For every registered animal, there are thousands of ordinarily respectable house cats, as well as legions of beatniks living in city alleys or country fields.

The "cat fancy"—cat dealers, breeders, and admirers— goes to great lengths to define the various breeds, and to keep the blood strains pure. This is often a discouraging business, for the aristocrats of catdom take no interest in such matters. The mating of dogs and other domestic animals can be controlled to some extent by their owners, but with cats this is a much more difficult task. Cats, if they have access to the outdoors, wander where they will, and take romance where they find it.

There have never been as strong reasons for developing new breeds of cats as is the case with dogs. Men have always needed different kinds of dogs for such various uses as hunting, herding, guarding, and the like. But for catching mice, one kind of cat is as good as another.

As cats have come more and more into favor as house pets, interest has increased in making them more beautiful. This interest has grown steadily with the passage of time. It has led to the development of new breeds, the introduction of foreign breeds, and the formation of cat clubs, whose members vie with one another in developing handsome specimens.

The exhibition of purebred cats in shows began in England in the 1870's. The first American show was held in 1895. These affairs have grown in popularity, and have come to be an annual event in many cities. They have had great influence in keeping breeds pure. Rigid standards of form and color are used by judges as a basis for determining the quality of entries. An owner whose cat wins the title "Best in Show" swells with pride, and gloats over the portrait of his champion in the newspapers. The beribboned champion, after the manner of cats, shows little interest and takes it all in stride.

Attempts to produce new breeds have met with only limited success, for reasons that have already been mentioned. Fanciers now confine their efforts largely to the perfection of color strains, improvement in the quality of the fur and conformity with standard show points.

The introduction of established breeds from foreign countries is quite another matter. This has been a great success. A good proportion of the entries at a present-day show belong to breeds that had their origin far away and long ago.

They are unusual in appearance and somewhat rare, qualities that always interest a crowd.

Ten breeds are generally recognized by the various cat clubs as eligible for entry in shows. Several others are being developed but are not yet officially on most lists. In addition to these, there is a class listed as Household Pets, in which only unpedigreed cats can be entered. In most shows, they do not compete against the purebred cats. A winner in this class is awarded the title "Best Household Pet."

The ten breeds most widely recognized are: Domestic Shorthair, Persian, Siamese, Burmese, Russian Blue, Abyssinian, Manx, Rex, Himalayan, and Havana Brown. Of these, only the Persian and the Himalayan are longhairs.

Shorthairs far outnumber longhairs as pets, but until recently Persians were the majority of entries in shows. Their owners claim that these are the aristocrats among cats, and make more spectacular exhibits than their shorthair cousins. This is perhaps true, but owners of shorthairs would never admit it. Doubtless all early domestic cats had short coats, like all wildcats. It is believed that Persians first appeared as a chance variation or mutation that has become fixed as a breed by mating Persian with Persian for many generations.

Here we will discuss the two recognized domestic breeds, Domestic Shorthairs and Persians. In the next chapter, we will look at the so-called fancy breeds.

DOMESTIC SHORTHAIR

This is the favorite and well loved family cat. Surely no other animal has an equal place in history, legend, song, and story. This is the cat that helped Dick Whittington become Lord Mayor of London; that was the persecuted partner of witches; that played the fiddle as the cow jumped over the moon. It was the hero of Puss-in-Boots; the grinning Cheshire Cat of *Alice in Wonderland;* and the cat that walked alone in Kipling's *Just So Stories.*

As we have seen, its lineage is believed to go back to the sacred cat of Egypt, crossed later with the European wildcat. Wherever restless man has wandered, he has taken his house pet along, so that now the breed is found in all parts of the world. Many millions of people have loved this animal, and a few here and there have hated it. It is safe to say that the famous cat haters of history were people we would not have enjoyed knowing. Louis XIV, the Sun King of France; Napoleon Bonaparte; Alexander the Great—all were men who hated any creature that would not come running when they called.

The Domestic Shorthair comes in an endless variety of patterns and colors, of which less than forty are recognized as standard. A cat of this breed may be all white or all black, or it may be marked with solid patches of both. Many, called tabbies, are striped or marbled. Other colors often appear, such as reddish or bluish. A cat with patches of

98

TORTOISE-SHELLS, *a variety of Domestic Shorthair.*

black, orange and cream is known as a tortoise-shell, and is almost always a female.

The eyes vary in color too. If a cat is all white, its eyes may be blue or copper-colored, or it may have one blue and one copper-colored eye. Completely black specimens are rare. Usually a black cat has a patch of white on its throat or chest. To be considered for championship, it must be without a single white hair, and have orange or copper eyes.

PERSIAN

These are the glamor boys of the cat world. They were formerly called Angoras, and that name is still used at times, though dyed-in-the-wool cat fanciers may wince when they hear it. It is doubtful that these cats came originally from Persia, though no one can say where they did come from. Angoras were a separate and distinct breed which is now rarely seen, and which was never recognized by the cat fancy. Whether the name comes from their fur's resemblance to that of the Angora goat, or whether they did really originate in the vicinity of Angora (Ankara) in Turkey, no one knows for sure.

Maine coon cats are a variant breed (probably of Angoras) that are not recognized for exhibition. Many of their owners believe they are a cross between cat and raccoon. This is not true. Such a cross would be impossible.

The chief distinction of the Persian is of course its luxuriant glossy coat. Certainly no cat is more beautiful. Show

standards recognize thirty color strains, and there is a specified eye color for each strain. The perfect Persian should have a chunky body, short legs, a deep chest, and massive shoulders and rump. With its long silky hair, it looks somewhat like a big powder puff.

Since they are very fashionable and glamorous, Persians are often owned by people who consider themselves very fashionable and glamorous. A promising kitten may cost several hundred dollars if it has many champions in its lineage. Living as they usually do in luxurious quarters, such aristocratic cats may have little opportunity to chase mice. But in parks and gardens they can still indulge their sporting instincts by catching butterflies and grasshoppers.

CHAPTER 10
More Aristocrats

The cats that get the lion's share of limelight at shows are the so-called "foreign breeds." This is a convenient name for a group that includes all show classes other than Domestic Shorthairs and Persians. Most of the breeds discussed below are fully recognized. The others are still in an experimental stage, and are not yet on the official list.

SIAMESE

Not all the cats in Siam (Thailand) belong to the breed that we know as Siamese. Cats there are as much of a mixture as they are anywhere else. But among the nobles and priests of this ancient kingdom, the "royal and sacred" variety has long been cultivated.

A Siamese female named "Mrs. Poodles" was exhibited in an English cat show in 1872. The breed did not become established, however, until 1884, when the King of Siam gave a pair as a parting gift to a British consul about to return home. He took them to England, where they soon began producing kittens. Some of their descendants were brought to America not long afterward. They were greatly admired by fanciers, and brought prices as high as $1000 each. Since then, their popularity has gone up—and their prices have gone down. They are still expensive to buy, however.

Siamese are by far the most numerous of all imported breeds, and now rival Persians in the number of exhibits at any cat show. Their appearance is so different from that of other cats that their lineage might be thought to be quite distinct from that of the Domestic Shorthair. However, early photographs of Siamese cats show that they closely resembled Domestic Shorthairs except in color. The differences in body type today are largely the result of selective breeding.

Show standards require the Siamese to be rather small, with slender body and thin, tapered tail. The head should be wedge-shaped, and the eyes narrow and slanted slightly downward toward the nose. Crossed eyes and kinked tails, both fairly common, are considered defects. There should be no tabby stripes on tail or legs, and the hindlegs should be a little longer than the forelegs.

A good Siamese has short, extremely fine fur. The most usual color is light tan. One other body color, grayish blue, is recognized. Outstanding features of this breed are its "points," meaning face (called the mask), ears, legs, feet, and

tail. The points are of a different and darker color than the rest of the body. Depending on the color of its points, a Siamese is called seal point (blackish brown), chocolate point, lilac point, or blue point. The last two colors appear only on specimens that have grayish blue bodies. Kittens are born almost white, and develop body color and dark points as they begin to mature.

These are very independent and active cats. They sometimes annoy owners by climbing up window curtains and screen doors to promenade along the tops of picture frames and high bookcases. Their voices are shriller than those of most cats, and sound raspy and harsh to some ears. Their

105

vocal talents may make them unwelcome pets for those who love a quiet home. But in the opinion of a host of admirers, their great beauty and grace more than make up for such minor annoyances.

BURMESE

This breed was developed in America rather recently. A female cat named Wong Mau was brought ashore at San Francisco by a sailor in 1930. A fancier, Doctor Joseph Thompson, admired its sleek brown coat so much that the sailor gave it to him. Doctor Thompson bred his new pet to a pedigreed Siamese, and some of the resulting kittens grew into lovely sable-brown, golden-eyed cats. Their descendants have been established as a breed that is rapidly gaining friends.

Next to the Persians and the Siamese, they have become the most popular of all cats other than the Domestic Short-hair. A Burmese rather resembles a small Domestic, but with shorter coat, rounder head, and solid brown coloring. The show standards specify stocky bodies, and a close-clinging, short coat that has a glossy sheen and satiny texture. The eyes must be yellow or golden, and as round as possible. Burmese are considered as "solid color" cats, with points no darker than the general body color, and all other marking and white hairs are outlawed. Kittens are born lighter than adults.

The voices of these cats are very soft and less frequently

used than those of their Siamese cousins. Many Burmese fanciers insist that their pets are unusually intelligent, but admirers of other breeds are likely to make the same claim for their own favorites. Unusually intelligent or not, Burmese are certainly unusually handsome.

RUSSIAN BLUE

Judging by the number of fancy breeds that are said to have originated in palaces, one would conclude that royal personages spend much of their time breeding cats. A case in point is the Russian Blue, reported to have come to America directly from the Imperial Palace in St. Petersburg. But in this case, at any rate, the story of a royal origin is not borne out by facts.

There have long been blue, or "Maltese," cats among house pets everywhere. But the particular breed now known as Russian Blue has been recognized in England only since the beginning of the present century. The first of the breed to be seen in America was imported from England in 1947.

The color is described in show standards as "bright blue." This is hardly an exact description. The color is really bluish-gray or light slate-gray. The common run of cat

RUSSIAN BLUE

owners might see no great difference between an imported Russian Blue and any well-bred bluish-gray house cat. But the fancier would notice the Russian Blue's bright green eyes, the Roman nose and the silver tip on each hair. This cat's color, now fixed by inbreeding, was no doubt originally a chance variation, such as may appear in any litter of variously colored kittens. An English cat expert, Brian Vesey-Fitzgerald, found in an English farmer's cottage a fine specimen of blue cat that had been born in the litter of a tortoise shell mother. When it grew up, an occasional blue kitten appeared among its numerous offspring.

The show standards of various cat groups differ somewhat for the breed. Most of them specify a broad face, round green eyes set widely apart, and large ears with pointed tips. The color must be uniform all over the body, and without tabby stripes or other markings. The fur should be short, thick, and silky, very much like sealskin.

ABYSSINIAN

This is another breed for which its more credulous friends claim a royal background. Some of its admirers believe that the Abyssinian once romped with the pet lions on the steps of the Imperial Palace in Addis Ababa.

While that may be true, it is certain that the first of the breed to be seen by western fanciers came from no royal palace. One account runs that the first specimens were brought to Europe in 1868 by a soldier who had served in a British campaign in Abyssinia (now called Ethiopia). According to another account, the breed originated in England about that time by mating selected short-haired house cats.

If the Aby did originate in Abyssinia, it may well be a modern edition of the sacred Egyptian cat. Both the Egyptian cat and the Aby could have stemmed from the same wild ancestor, the African Kaffir cat, which is found in both Egypt and Abyssinia. The general characteristics of the Aby and the Egyptian are certainly similar. This becomes apparent when we compare an Abyssinian with the mummy of an Egyptian. Of course a live cat is much more beautiful than any mummy, but in life the Egyptian must have looked very much like a modern Aby.

The outstanding feature of this breed is its "ticked" fur. This cat fancier's word means that each hair is marked with two or three bands of different color, running from silver next to the skin through various shades of brown and black. This unique coloration makes its wearer appear at a distance to be a short-haired, light brown cat. When examined closely, the dark and light ticking makes its fur resemble the pepper-and-salt coat of a cottontail rabbit.

The Abyssinian is a long-recognized breed. Show standards specify a tall, slender body, rather small head, long neck, and large, pointed ears. The eyes should be almond shaped, and colored green, yellow, or hazel. The small, neat feet have black pads, and the same color should extend up the back of the legs.

The perfect Aby must have a long, tapered tail, with a faint dark line running along it to a black tip. There should be no tabby stripes or other markings on the body. No white is allowed except a small area under the chin.

These are often nervous cats. They may pace restlessly if confined in a cage, and move with hair-trigger suddenness when disturbed. There is a strong strain of wildness in their makeup, and they indulge in much rough and tumble play.

111

MANX

Show rules specify few hard-and-fast requirements for Manx cats. This class must have well rounded rumps, supported on hindlegs longer than forelegs. They may wear fur of any body color, but it must be a double coat: a thick, close-lying under layer, with an outer guard of longer hairs. The color of the eyes must conform to coat color as specified for Domestic Shorthairs and Persians.

But no cat may be entered in a show as a Manx if it has even the stump of a tail. Preferably, there should be a decided hollow at the end of the backbone, where the tails of other cats begin.

There have been plenty of absurd explanations as to how Manx cats came by this embarrassing peculiarity. On the Isle of Man, which lies between England and Ireland, a legend runs that it all began in 1588. At that time, storms drove a ship of the Spanish Armada on a reef off the coast of the island. From the sinking vessel, a tailless tomcat swam ashore, where it lived to father many litters of tailless kittens. The story neglects to explain the presence of such a curiosity aboard a ship of Spain, a country where there is no record of tailless cats.

Or you may prefer the explanation of an old rhyme, which suggests that the cats of Man may have worn off their tails "by sedentary habits, as do the rabbits." In another story, Father Noah is blamed for an unfortunate accident that was responsible for the loss. In his haste to set sail on his famous

112

MANX

voyage, Noah suddenly closed the door of the Ark before the cat had quite got aboard.

But we cannot accept such fascinating explanations. In the opinion of unimaginative scientists, the taillessness of the Manx breed had its origin simply as another of those chance mutations that occur in all animal species. Tailless cats are found in many widely separated countries, especially in the

Far East. Burma, Siam, Malaysia, as well as China and Japan, all have them. It is extremely doubtful that the Manx cat originated in the Isle of Man. In some unknown way, this unique animal was established and spread widely on that island, so the name has been applied to all tailless cats.

This is not really a true breed. The special characteristics of a true breed must hold through generation after generation, and this is not the case with the special characteristic of the Manx. Almost all Manx litters contain one or more kittens with tails. And a tailless kitten may occur now and then in a litter of any breed.

But so far as show standards go, Manx cats are a recognized class that is judged by specified regulations. They do not seem to be any the worse for the lack of a tail, a member which, after all, is of little use to a cat. At any rate, they do not have to suffer the indignity of having their tails accidentally stepped on.

This brings to mind another folktale of the Isle of Man. Some superstitious Manxmen believe that anyone who steps on a cat's tail will soon be bitten by a snake. When a tailless cat happened to be born ages ago on the island, the owner at once recognized its advantages. He could move about as carelessly as he pleased without treading on his cat's tail and thus exposing himself to the danger of snake bite. Ever since, so the story goes, Manxmen have bred their cats from the original tailless strain and have, one assumes, avoided the dire consequences of a careless step.

REX

REX and HAVANA BROWN

The Rex has short, curly hair which grows in graceful waves along the sides and tail. It looks like the fur known as Persian lamb, and may be of any color. This handsome curiosity is now recognized by all cat groups. A curly-haired kitten born in England and one born in Germany are the founders of the strain. Their offspring are being bred in an attempt to establish a curly-haired breed.

The Havana Brown is a short-haired cat with rich chestnut brown coat and green eyes. A recognized class in all shows, it has a muscular body with a coat somewhat shorter and redder than the Burmese.

HIMALAYAN

HIMALAYAN and BALINESE

The Himalayan breed resembles the Siamese in the color and pattern of its coat, but it has the Persian type of body and long, wavy hair. The eyes are blue. The breed was developed by crossing the Persian and the Siamese.

A breed similar in appearance to the Himalayan is the Balinese. It too was developed from a Siamese-Persian cross. The Siamese characteristics predominate in body-type and color, but it has the long coat of the Persian. The breed is recognized in many shows, but not all.

116

KORAT and COLOR POINT SHORTHAIR

The unrecognized breed called Korat comes from Siam, where it is native to a section of that country known as the Korat Plateau. It is built like a Siamese, but is solid slate-gray in color, with silvery legs and green eyes.

The Color Point Shorthair is a cross between variously colored Domestic Shorthairs and the Siamese. It is not well established as yet, but its breeders are working to produce a cat with the color pattern and build of a Siamese, and points either red, tortoise shell, or tabby marked. In some shows, these cats can compete as Siamese, but in others they are in a division by themselves.

From all this, you will gather that there is a wide area of choice if you are planning to go in for cat breeding. There is a cat to please every taste. But you must decide on your own judgment as to which kitten to choose. Not all the members of any particular breed are likely to develop the characteristics that you look for in a pet. There are good cats and bad cats in every breed.

If you base your choice on appearance, you have a tremendous variety to pick from: cats of almost any color, long-haired cats, curly-haired cats, short-haired cats. You could even have chosen, some years ago, a cat without any hair at all, the Mexican Hairless. This breed has died out, perhaps because it could find nobody to love it.

CHAPTER 11

The Mind of the Cat

Aesop, author of the famous fables, wrote about animals as if they were human beings, crediting them with all the mental accomplishments of men. They loved and hated, were treacherous or loyal, shrewd or silly, sly or straightforward. Aesop of course made no pretense at writing natural history. But too many serious students of natural history, in more recent times, have made the mistake of crediting animals with too great a share of man's mental abilities.

In reaction, many present-day scientists have gone to the opposite extreme. They hold that all animal activities are based on purely mechanical instinct.

Ordinary people who have a natural liking for animals usually hold a less extreme opinion on this matter. They have pets in their homes, are sympathetic with them, and have daily opportunity to observe their traits. Any person

119

who owns a well-loved cat can point to numerous incidents that prove, to his own satisfaction at least, that his pet has some ability to think. Especially devoted cat owners are prone to go further than this, and maintain that their particular favorites have mental abilities that sometimes approach genius.

Perhaps we shall come nearer to the truth if we favor a middle ground between the extreme scientific view and the opinion of the over-enthusiastic pet owner.

Professional naturalists have long been concerned principally with the physical make-up of animals, and the relation of one species with another. The few naturalists who were interested in mental traits carried on their studies largely by means of contrived laboratory tests. These consisted of simple problems which the animals being studied were encouraged to solve in order to gain a reward of food.

For example, a hungry cat might be confined in a cage, with a tempting meal in sight through the bars. If it pulled a cord dangling inside its prison, the door would fly open, allowing the occupant to walk out and eat the food. The idea was to find out how quickly, or how slowly, the prisoner would learn that pulling the cord would cause the door to open. The length of time it took the cat to learn the trick by trial and error furnished a measure of its intelligence. Having once opened the door, the animal might again be put into the closed cage after an hour or so. Then its promptness or slowness in pulling the cord would show how well it remembered the knowledge it had gained in the first test. Little consideration was given to whether the subject was hungry, whether it liked the food offered, whether it took time out to lick its fur, or whether it just liked being in the cage.

Tests of this kind led most scientists to conclude that even the "higher" animals possess no reasoning ability whatever. All their actions were held to be ruled by inherited instinct, without any exercise of what we know as thought.

This low rating of the mental equipment of animals has been modified somewhat in recent years by a group of naturalists known as *behaviorists*. These men are interested primarily in finding out why animals behave as they do, rather than in the physical make-up of their bodies. Many behaviorists believe that such studies can best be carried on by observing their subjects in the field under the natural conditions of their daily lives. Captive animals do not behave as they do when free, and their actions often are influenced by the confusion necessarily caused by laboratory experiments.

Behaviorists have come to believe that at least the higher animals do understand, to a certain degree, the principle of cause and effect—that pulling the cord is the *cause* that brings about the *effect* of the door's opening. Their experiments also show that animals remember and profit by former experience. Having once learned how to open the door, does a cat, on its second imprisonment, remember its lesson?

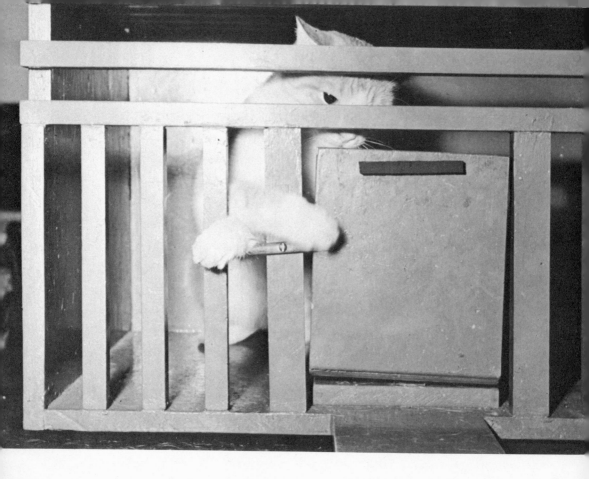

Experiments have shown that many animals do remember, at least for a short time, and on the second test, open the door more promptly than on the first. An especially quick learner may open it at once. The dolts may never learn. There are smart cats and dull cats, just as there are brilliant and slow students in any school.

A noted British naturalist, St. George Mivart, in his classic study *The Cat*, describes an incident that seems to show that a cat solved a rather knotty problem by thinking. This animal repeatedly tried to catch a starling from a flock feed-ing in a meadow. Whenever the stealthy hunter crept near, the flock took fright and flew away, only to return when the cat went back to its hiding place. A cow was also feeding in the meadow, at times grazing in the midst of the flock without disturbing them in the least. At length it happened to come near the hidden cat, which jumped onto the ani-mal's back and crouched there quietly. When the cow's grazing again led her among the birds, the cat suddenly leaped to the ground and easily captured its dinner.

It would seem evident that this cat realized, by some sort of mental process, that the starlings were not disturbed by the cow's grazing among them. It sensed that if it mounted the grazing animal secretly and lay low, it would in time be carried near enough to the birds to pounce on one of them.

After much consideration of feline mental ability, Mivart concludes, "We cannot, without becoming cats, perfectly understand the cat's mind."

Needless to say, no human being—not even a witch—has ever become a cat. But men have always been curious about whatever they did not understand. And their curiosity about the cat's mind has led to some widely differing judgments. Various naturalists have "proved," after long and complicated experiments, that cats are very smart—or very stupid. That they are sensitive to color—or totally color-blind. That they learn readily—or never learn to recognize even their own names. That they can reason to some extent—or that they do everything by instinct. The unscientific friend of cats finds it difficult to choose among such contradictory conclusions.

Even though he may have love and sympathy for animals, the scientist must regard them simply as subjects for his experiments, and purposely avoid any sentiment toward them. Those who keep cats because they like them, and observe them day after day in friendly association, believe that many of their actions result from some exercise of intelligence.

Everyone would agree that many things cats do are the result of pure instinct. For example, a newborn kitten soon discovers the place where it can find milk. When an enemy appears, a cat makes use of its instinctive defenses: to run, to hide, to climb a tree, or to fight if cornered.

But cats often modify their instinctive actions by an intelligent adjustment to the facts of their lives. They usually treat dogs as enemies, yet many a cat lives in complete harmony with the dog that lives in the same household. The cat's natural prey is the rodent, yet cats have been known to nurse and rear rats and mice.

Do cats have a language? We are so used to the idea of spoken language that we are likely to forget that there are other ways to communicate thoughts.

A beloved nature writer, John Burroughs, once expressed the opinion that no animal can think. "You cannot think," said he, "without a language, and animals do not have a language." Of course animals do not communicate by

A kitten and a mouse may make friends.

spoken words, as we do. An intelligent dog can be taught to recognize the meaning of perhaps seventy-five words, but no dog has ever learned to talk. Some birds, such as parrots and crows, learn to pronounce certain words, but they only imitate sounds they have heard. They have no idea of using words to make their wants known. A young chimpanzee named Vicki was once taught, after more than two years' effort, to make noises that sounded something like "papa" and "cup." Eventually she learned to say "cup" when she wanted a drink of water. You cannot carry on a conversation with a vocabulary of two words.

But there are many ways of expressing thoughts other than by the spoken word. A human speaker's meaning is always shown partly by his gestures, and by the tone of his voice.

Animals do have a language, of their own sort. They communicate with one another and with human beings by means of sounds and gestures, some of which serve the same purpose that human language serves to men. When a cat is at ease, it purrs. If it is in pain, it squalls. When it carries its tail high, it is healthy, or content. When it is afraid, the tail is curled underneath its body. The gestures it makes with its paws have meaning. Such sounds and actions are its means of expression.

Carl Van Vechten, in his book *The Tiger in the House,* tells of a hungry vagabond cat that was once fed a good meal at the back door of a farmhouse. Next day it appeared at the same door, followed by twenty-nine hungry companions! How it told its friends about the prospect of a handout can only be guessed, but it had certainly spread the news in some way.

Among animals, the need to communicate does not cover a wide range. Their needs consist almost entirely in conveying wants and emotions. And their limited means of expression serve to do this very well. A man who wants to enter a locked door knocks or rings a bell or calls to some-one who has a key. A cat produces the same result by stand-ing at the door and miaowing. Both means of communication succeed in getting the door open.

Cats have no conception of such human ideas as kindness, cruelty, honesty, generosity, or selfishness. Their actions cannot be judged by human standards, which are the only standards we know. No cat is concerned with behaving like a human being.

Many people are shocked at the cat's habit of toying with a captured bird or mouse. This seems to us to be a cruel proceeding, but to the cat it serves as valuable practice to keep in trim for future hunting. Bird watchers are distressed by the cat's eternal war on their feathered friends. They fail to consider the fact that all cats have been hunters since time began. This is the cat's way of life, which all cats must necessarily follow. You can never break the habit by pun-ishing the hunter when it drops a captured bird at your feet. The cat cannot conceive any wrongdoing in its act.

A tired businessman, awakened from much-needed sleep by a tomcat's wild screeching, is apt to curse the entire feline tribe, and throw an old shoe at the offender. To another tom, the unearthly caterwauling is an exciting challenge, a defiance of his own prowess. To the cat ear, it is not a discordant shriek, any more than the skirling of the bagpipes is discordant to the ears of a Scottish regiment going into battle.

There is a tendency among some people to say that all cats are furtive, disdainful, or have some other failing objectionable by human standards. You cannot generalize about cats; they are individualists. There is no particular quality of mind or character that is common to all cats, or to all members of a particular breed. A possible exception is the Siamese, which is notoriously given to noise making. Between the individual members of all breeds, there are great differences. Even kittens of the same litter may develop into adults that are quite unlike one another in character.

Many cats show strong likes or dislikes for certain persons. In any household, the house pet may show special fondness for one member of the family, and merely tolerate the others. Cats have no feeling that it would be polite to distribute their favors impartially.

There are numerous mysteries of the feline mind that we cannot fathom. One of the most mysterious is the cat's ability to find its way home when released at a great distance. This ability, known as homing instinct, is possessed by many other animals. Homing pigeons are especially noted for this talent. They find their way back to an accustomed roost when released many miles away from it.

Many authentic stories are on record of cats that have returned to a favored home from a far-distant spot. A remarkable example is reported in a newspaper despatch from the town of Seminole, Oklahoma. The story concerns a female cat named Thrum. Early in December, 1964, her owner moved from Seminole to a new home in St. Louis, 450 miles away, making the trip by automobile with the cat in the car. After a short stay in the new location Thrum disappeared. Six weeks later, she turned up at the old home of her mistress in Seminole.

Whether or not we can understand the cat's mind, we can all understand and appreciate her charm. She is a beautiful, graceful creature, a model house guest, and an affectionate companion. Do not be offended if she does not always respond to your friendly advances. The cat is an independent citizen of a world of her own. You cannot dominate her, or make her your slave. She is a creature of many moods, and receives or bestows affection when it suits her own convenience.

She is modest, clean, and dignified. There are many qualities of her character that would grace any human being. If she is in the mood, she gives you a slight token of affection by rubbing herself against your leg. If she happens to be in a warmer mood, she jumps into your lap and nuzzles your cheek, purring softly. If she is so minded, she lies quietly by the fire, or goes silently about her own affairs.

No other animals that have lived in intimate association with man have experienced such dramatic variations in his regard for them. The cat has been deified, persecuted, loved, and feared. But she has come through all these ups and downs with undaunted spirit, to win a firm and lasting place in the hearts of man. She fills a basic human need for things other than material.

Amid the anxieties of modern life, man needs the restful companionship of friendly animals. This need is well filled by the cat, the most beautifully perfect of all the animal kingdom.

Appendix

THE CAT'S FAMILY TREE

Dog family

Raccoon family

Bear family

Weasel family

The present time

10 million years ago

20 million years ago

30 million years ago

40 million years ago

Miacis

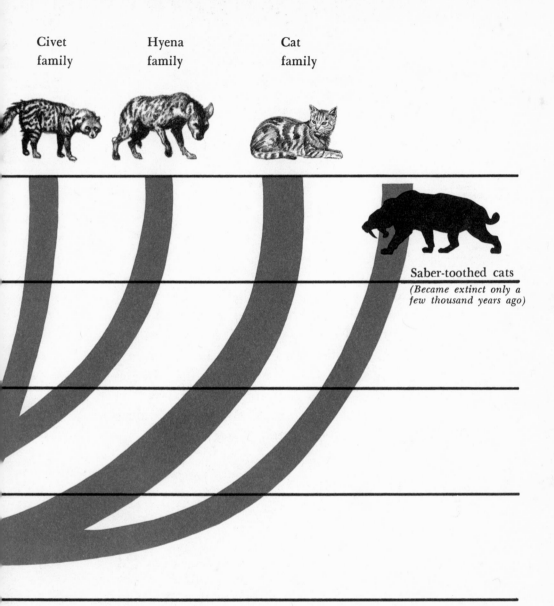

Civet
family

Hyena
family

Cat
family

Saber-toothed cats
(Became extinct only a few thousand years ago)

Chart showing the probable evolution
of cats and other carnivorous mammals
from a common ancestor, *Miacis*

THE CAT FAMILY
Genera and Species

The various species of the cat family (Felidae) are so similar in anatomy that there is considerable difference of opinion as to their proper classification. The classification given here follows the one used by Lee S. Crandall, General Curator Emeritus of the New York Zoological Park, in *Management of Wild Mammals in Captivity* (University of Chicago Press, 1964); by Ellerman and Morrison-Scott in *Checklist of Palaearctic and Indian Mammals* (British Museum, 1951); and by George Gaylord Simpson in *The Principles of Classification and a Classification of Mammals* (Bulletin of the American Museum of Natural History, 1945).

COMMON NAME	TECHNICAL NAME	OLD OR NEW WORLD
Species of the Genus *Panthera*		
Clouded leopard	*Panthera nebulosa*	Old
Jaguar	*Panthera onca*	New
Leopard	*Panthera pardus*	Old
Lion	*Panthera leo*	Old
Snow leopard	*Panthera uncia*	Old
Tiger	*Panthera tigris*	Old

COMMON NAME	TECHNICAL NAME	OLD OR NEW WORLD
Species of the Genus *Acinonyx*		
Cheetah	*Acinonyx jubatus*	Old
Species of the Genus *Felis*		
African golden cat	*Felis aurata*	Old
Andean cat	*Felis jacobita*	New
Black-footed cat	*Felis nigripes*	Old
Bobcat (American wildcat)	*Felis rufa*	New
Bornean red cat	*Felis badia*	Old
Caracal	*Felis caracal*	Old
Chinese desert cat	*Felis bieti*	Old
Domestic cat	*Felis catus*	Old and New
European wildcat (Scottish wildcat)	*Felis silvestris*	Old
Fishing cat	*Felis viverrina*	Old
Flat-headed cat	*Felis planiceps*	Old
Geoffroy's cat	*Felis geoffroyi*	New
Jaguarundi	*Felis yagouarundi*	New
Jungle cat	*Felis chaus*	Old
Kaffir cat (African wildcat)	*Felis libyca*	Old
Kodkod	*Felis guigna*	New
Leopard cat	*Felis bengalensis*	Old
Little spotted cat	*Felis tigrina*	New
Lynx	*Felis lynx*	Old and New
Marbled cat	*Felis marmorata*	Old
Margay	*Felis wiedi*	New
Ocelot	*Felis pardalis*	New
Pallas's cat	*Felis manul*	Old
Pampas cat	*Felis colocolo*	New
Puma (cougar, mountain lion)	*Felis concolor*	New
Rusty-spotted cat	*Felis rubiginosa*	Old
Sand cat	*Felis margarita*	Old
Serval	*Felis serval*	Old
Temminck's cat	*Felis temmincki*	Old

BIBLIOGRAPHY

* Chandoha, Walter. *Walter Chandoha's Book of Kittens and Cats*. New York: Citadel Press, 1963.

* Colbert, Edwin H. "Where the Cats Came From," *The Illustrated Library of the Natural Sciences*, Vol. I. New York: Simon and Schuster, 1958.

   Crandall, Lee S. *Management of Wild Mammals in Captivity*. Chicago: University of Chicago Press, 1964.

* Denis, Armand. *Cats of the World*. Boston: Houghton Mifflin Company, 1964.

   Howey, M. Oldfield. *The Cat in the Mysteries of Religion and Magic*. New York: Castle Books, 1956.

* Lockridge, Frances and Richard. *Cats and People*. Philadelphia & New York: J. B. Lippincott Co., 1950.

* McNulty, Faith, and Keiffer, Elizabeth. *Wholly Cats*. New York & Indianapolis: The Bobbs-Merrill Company, 1962.

   Mery, Fernand. *Her Majesty the Cat*. New York: Criterion Books, 1950.

   Mivart, St. George. *The Cat*. London: John Murray, 1881.

   Repplier, Agnes. *Fireside Sphinx*. Boston: Houghton Mifflin Company, 1939.

   Sanderson, Ivan T. *Living Mammals of the World*. Garden City: Hanover House.

   Scott, John Paul. *Animal Behavior*. Chicago: University of Chicago Press, 1958.

   Stanek, V. J. *Introducing the Cat Family*. London: Spring Books.

* Suehsdorf, Adolph. "The Cats in Our Lives," *National Geographic Magazine,* April, 1964.

Van Vechten, Carl. *The Tiger in the House.* New York: Alfred A. Knopf, 1920.

* Webster, Gary. "Majesty in a Fur Coat," *The Illustrated Library of the Natural Sciences,* Vol. I. New York: Simon and Schuster, 1958.

* Winslow, Helen M. *Concerning Cats.* Boston: Lothrop Publishing Company, 1900.

Zeuner, Frederick E. *A History of Domesticated Animals.* New York: Harper & Row, 1963.

---

* *Particularly recommended for readers of this book.*

Index

ABOUT THE AUTHOR

Carl Burger's lifelong interest in animals began when he was a boy growing up in the mountains of eastern Tennessee.

Trained as an architect at Cornell University, Mr. Burger also studied painting at the School of the Museum of Fine Arts in Boston, and taught in the School of Architecture at the University of Illinois. During World War I, he served as a captain of infantry in France.

Since 1920 he has lived and worked as an illustrator near New York City. He is the author-illustrator of several books about animals, and the illustrator of many others, including *The Incredible Journey, Old Yeller, Savage Sam,* and *Familiar Animals of America.*

ALLABOUT BOOKS BY CARL BURGER

All About Fish with a foreword by James W. Atz, Associate Curator, New York Aquarium. Illustrated by the author.

All About Dogs with a foreword by Lee S. Crandall, General Curator Emeritus, New York Zoological Park. Illustrated with photographs and with drawings by the author.

All About Elephants with a foreword by Fairfield Osborn, President, New York Zoological Society. Illustrated with photographs and with drawings by the author.

All About Cats with a foreword by William Bridges, Curator of Publications (Retired), New York Zoological Society. Illustrated with photographs.